BALLET MUSIC

The Blue Birds (from "The Sleeping Beauty")

BALLET MUSIC

by

ROGER FISKE

AUTHOR OF " LISTENING TO MUSIC "

Illustrated with photographs

GEORGE G. HARRAP AND COMPANY LTD
LONDON   TORONTO   WELLINGTON   SYDNEY

For

ALISON

ACKNOWLEDGMENTS

ACKNOWLEDGMENTS are due to the following for permission to reproduce illustrations and music : Tony Armstrong-Jones, for a picture of *The Prince of the Pagodas;* Baron, for pictures of *Coppélia* (p. 27), *Swan Lake* (p. 41), and *Daphnis and Chloe;* Boosey and Hawkes, Ltd, for excerpts from *Petrushka* and *The Prince of the Pagodas;* J. and W. Chester, Ltd, for excerpts from *The Firebird;* Mike Davis, for two pictures of *Nutcracker;* Dominic, for a picture of *Petrushka* (p. 65); Durand et Cie, Paris (United Music Publishers, Ltd, London), for excerpts from *Daphnis and Chloe;* Felix Fonteyn, for a picture of *Sylvia;* Houston Rogers, for a picture of *Swan Lake* (p. 38); Hurok Attractions, Inc., New York, for a picture of *The Sleeping Beauty;* Edward Mandinian, for a picture of *Job;* Denis de Marney, for a picture of *Coppélia,* (p. 24); the Oxford University Press, Ltd, for excerpts from *Job;* J. Arthur Rank, Ltd, for a picture of *Giselle;* and Roger Wood, for a picture of *Petrushka* (p. 67).

First published in Great Britain 1958
by GEORGE G. HARRAP *&* CO. LTD
182 High Holborn, London, W.C.1

© *Roger Fiske* 1958

Composed in Baskerville type and printed and bound by the Hollen Street Press Ltd, London, W.1
Made in Great Britain

CONTENTS

CHAPTER   PAGE

1. MUSIC IN THE BACKGROUND   7

2. EARLY BALLET MUSIC   10

3. ADAM AND THE ROMANTIC BALLET   14
    Giselle

4. DELIBES AND THE FRENCH BALLET   22
    Coppélia
    Sylvia

5. TCHAIKOVSKY AND THE CLASSICAL BALLET   35
    Swan Lake
    The Sleeping Beauty
    Nutcracker

6. STRAVINSKY AND THE DIAGHILEV BALLET   58
    The Firebird
    Petrushka

7. SOME MODERN BALLETS   69
    Daphnis and Chloe
    Job
    The Prince of the Pagodas

8. CODETTA   86

    APPENDIX:
    LIST OF RECORDINGS   88

ILLUSTRATIONS

	PAGE
THE BLUE BIRDS (*The Sleeping Beauty*)	*Frontispiece*
GISELLE AND ALBRECHT (*Giselle*)	16
SWANILDA WATCHES AS FRANTZ MAKES ADVANCES TO COPPÉLIA (*Coppélia*)	24
DR COPPÉLIUS SURPRISES SWANILDA AND HER FRIENDS IN HIS WORKSHOP (*Coppélia*)	27
THE CORTÈGE RUSTIQUE (*Sylvia*)	32
ODETTE AND SIEGFRIED (*Swan Lake*)	38
ODILE DANCES WITH SIEGFRIED, WHILE ROTHBART LOOKS ON (*Swan Lake*)	41
THE BATTLE OF THE TOY SOLDIERS AND THE MICE (*Nutcracker*)	53
THE CHINESE DANCE FROM THE DIVERTISSEMENT (*Nutcracker*)	56
THE BLACKAMOOR, THE BALLERINA, AND PETRUSHKA (*Petrushka*)	65
THE BALLERINA ENTERS THE BLACKAMOOR'S ROOM (*Petrushka*)	67
DAPHNIS AND CHLOE (*Daphnis and Chloe*)	72
SATAN BEFORE GOD (SCENE I) (*Job*)	76
BELLE ROSE AND THE SALAMANDER (*The Prince of the Pagodas*)	80

Chapter One

MUSIC IN THE BACKGROUND

This book is about music specially written for ballet. Many modern ballets, and most of the shorter ones, are based on music that was never intended for dancing: these will not be discussed here. But all full-length ballets providing a whole evening's entertainment have had special music written for them, and so have a number of medium-length ballets; all the more important examples in the repertoire of British companies are discussed in the pages that follow.

It is noticeable that in the numerous books that have been written about ballet the music is seldom mentioned. This is because many of the people interested in ballet, on both sides of the footlights, do not consider the music very important. Dancers naturally think that they themselves are the chief attraction, and so, of course, they are. Many of those who are thrilled by Fonteyn or Beriosova or John Gilpin scarcely hear the music at all as they respond to the miraculous grace and agility being displayed on the stage. This attitude is reflected in the history of ballet. Whereas operas in the late eighteenth and in the nineteenth centuries were usually written by distinguished composers, ballet music was usually written by hacks whose names have long been forgotten; any music was good enough for ballet music. There are many great names in nineteenth-century ballet—Taglioni, Grisi, Elssler, for instance—but you have to search the museums to discover what music they danced to.

Within living memory a famous British ballet company has been known to devise a ballet to a well-known piece of orchestral music and then at the last moment switch to a completely different piece of music, with surprisingly little inconvenience to anyone. This attitude—that "any music will do"—is not often to be met with to-day in the ballet world; if it were there would be no point in writing this book. But it is true to say that the composer normally has much less control over the end-product than the composer of operas. Verdi and Puccini used to bully their librettists until they got what they wanted, and Wagner decided that the only way to get what he wanted was to write his libretti himself. But when Tchaikovsky wrote *The Sleeping Beauty* he was in no position to bully anyone; the choreographer, Marius Petipa, was in control. That is as it should be, for composers may know enough about singing to write an opera unaided, but they seldom or never know enough about dancing to write a ballet unaided. Petipa had read the fairy tale in a famous version by the French writer, Perrault; he roughed out a scenario (arranging the incidents in a suitable way for dancing), divided the scenario into actual dances, and even decided how many bars long each should be and what mood the music should be in.

But although the dancers and their steps seem, at the time, more important than the music to which they dance, history does much to reverse the position, for it is the music that survives and not the steps. Great progress has been made in the last few years in notating steps—that is, in putting down on paper sufficient indications to enable future dancers to repeat the steps of present-day dancers; also, filming a ballet can help to preserve steps for posterity. But ballets of the eighteenth and nineteenth centuries did not enjoy these advantages. No one knows what steps were danced to Mozart's *Les Petits Riens* or Beethoven's *Prometheus*, and if these ballets are re-staged, with newly-invented dances, the result is not a revival but a new ballet to old music (of which there are more than enough already). Often the music earns a new life on its own account. The dances from Purcell's *The Fairy Queen* and the ballet music from Schubert's *Rosamunde* are known to countless listeners, although the long-forgotten dancers who moved to this music at its first performance must have regarded it as a very subsidiary part of the entertainment.

Despite such examples, it was rare for a reputable composer to be asked to write ballet music before the 1870's, when Delibes wrote *Coppélia* (1870) and Tchaikovsky wrote *Swan Lake* (1875). Great dancers were legion in the nineteenth century, great ballet music a rarity. Not until Diaghilev brought his troupe of Russian dancers to Western Europe in 1909 did artistic circles here begin to take ballet music seriously. With the success (just before the First World War) of Diaghilev's 'house' composer, Stravinsky, in such works as *The Firebird* and *Petrushka*, it became fashionable and natural for distinguished composers to turn their attention to this new field, and whereas in the nineteenth century scarcely any great composers wrote ballet music, in the twentieth, thanks largely to Diaghilev, scarcely any great composer has not done so. The result has been an immense improvement in musical standards in the world of ballet, and an end of the theory that any music will do. With this improvement has come the rediscovery of the great ballets of the past—great because their music is great. It needed the Sadler's Wells company to reveal to the Western world the greatness of *Swan Lake* and *The Sleeping Beauty*. These ballets had not survived in the repertoire of any company outside Russia (where they have never been forgotten). To make possible the Sadler's Wells revivals, elderly Russian *émigrés* struggled to call up from their memories the steps that were danced on the stages of St Petersburg in the 1890's, and, thanks to their efforts, the traditions are established and can be preserved into the future.

And yet in many ways the survival of ballet music is a haphazard business. Far less is known about the great ballet music of the nineteenth century than about the great opera music. Ballet companies have long traded on this ignorance, inserting into works that must have been conceived as artistic wholes inappropriate music by other composers. Few people who go to Covent Garden know or care that some of the music they hear in *Giselle* is not by Adam, or that some of the music in *Swan Lake* consists of piano pieces by Tchaikovsky, orchestrated by an indifferent composer called Drigo. It is often very hard to discover who did write a particular piece which has long been accepted as part of a well-known ballet. And yet no one at Covent Garden would dream of inserting vocal versions of Tchaikovsky piano pieces into his operas—*Eugen Onegin*, for instance—or songs which were not by Verdi into a Verdi opera. Musicologists have not yet penetrated the ballet world; they will find plenty to occupy them when they do.

For years music critics accepted what they were offered because they had no means of checking up on what the composer actually wrote. Just after the War, when the Covent Garden production of *The Sleeping Beauty* was in its heyday, it was impossible to buy either a full score or a piano arrangement of the ballet anywhere in London. Again, the contrast with the world of opera is striking. More recently much has been done to remedy the situation. The Russian State publishing houses have produced definitive full scores of *The Sleeping Beauty* and *Nutcracker*, and one of *Swan Lake* is presumably on the way. But as regards the great French ballets the situation remains chaotic. There are no published full scores or orchestral parts of *Giselle*, *Coppélia*, or *Sylvia*, and there never have been. Piano arrangements of all three were printed, probably in time for their first performances, and can still be obtained, but no one in nineteenth-century Paris saw any reason for a full score. In the world of ballet at that time the conductor was not capable of following anything more complicated than a first violin part and did not expect anything better. Thus, what might be called the original source material of nineteenth-century ballets is often unobtainable in this country (does it exist in Paris?), and what there is has usually been bedevilled by choreographers cutting and adding without reference to the original composer.

A very similar situation existed in English opera houses in the early years of the nine-teenth century. Mozart's operas were unmercifully hacked about, and poor music by poor composers was inserted irrelevantly and irreverently. But opera people had put their house in order by the 1850's, or comparatively so. Operatic music was being treated with respect for three-quarters of a century before it occurred to anyone that a similar attitude to ballet music might not be unreasonable. Things are much better than they were, but there is still plenty of room for improvement on both sides of the footlights.

This book has been written in the belief that the ballet-lover who is swept away by the dancing will find even greater pleasure if he can divert some small part of his attention to the music. I must not put the claims of the music too high. The star ballerina and the poetry of her movements must always be the chief attraction. But there is much more in the music than meets the average ear. The composer may try to establish poetic moods and dramatic tensions and help the dancers to make the story clear. He may characterize the leading personages by associating a particular tune or tunes with each of them, as far as possible devising tunes that express their personalities in sound. Most of the audience will only be aware of such subtleties subconsciously. But how much more enjoyable to be able to appreciate them consciously! All opera-goers know that Wagner's operas are full of these *leitmotivs*, as they are called, and there have been many books explaining them. No one, as far as I know, has ever pointed out that almost all ballets (all but one of those dis-cussed in this book) have leitmotivs too, and there is no book giving information about them. Sometimes ballet companies themselves seem unaware of the composer's intentions in this respect, just failing to make the entrance of a character coincide with the playing of his tune by the orchestra.

You cannot really enjoy ballet, any more than you can opera, if you ignore the orchestra. The amount of attention you wish to give it will vary from moment to moment, and from ballet to ballet. It can even happen that the music is more interesting than the dancing. As far as I am concerned, this is true of both Ravel's *Daphnis and Chloe* and Vaughan Williams's *Job*; indeed, it is perhaps a fault in these ballets that the music is too assertively good (a fault that becomes an asset in the concert-hall), distracting too much of one's atten-tion from the stage. On the other hand, the music of *Giselle* has often been criticized for having too little to offer the ear, though in the theatre I am seldom aware of this alleged deficiency. Without any doubt the ideal, the middle course, the best of both worlds, is achieved by Tchaikovsky, and to some extent by Delibes and Stravinsky. Their music never makes you feel that the dancing is merely irrelevant decoration, and yet it will repay study and stand up on its own account in the concert-hall and on the gramophone record.

There remains the great problem: can one concentrate on two things at once? Can one watch and listen at the same time? This book is intended to help you to listen at any rate some of the time, and also to help those who live far from a theatre to love ballet music on the gramophone. And in case this book should be used in schools, I have given the words of some of the song-tunes ballet composers have introduced into their music, so that they can be sung; the words may even be of some interest to the general reader.

Chapter Two
EARLY BALLET MUSIC

The history of ballet has been told many times by people far more fitted to write of it than I am. In a book such as this there is no need to do more than indicate a few signposts and touch here and there on the musical side of early ballets. There is some excuse for the expected neglect of the music by ballet historians, for information is very hard to come by. Did Lully ever add eight bars to a dance at the request of a choreographer or write music in a given mood on demand? We do not know, but one can guess that in early days the composer had a good deal more control than he had by the latter half of the eighteenth century, by which time the star system was becoming established, and the composer was usually a nonentity, writing what he was told.

Ballet is usually said to have begun in France in 1581, though there had been primitive stage dancing before that. It seems that the orchestra was developing at this time, and was perhaps an essential ingredient in ballet as opposed to stage dancing. An orchestra can be defined as an ensemble in which—in some cases—more than one person plays the same instrumental part. Thus, if the composer writes five individual instrumental parts, and five players perform them, the result is chamber music. But if ten players perform them, two to each part, the result is orchestral music. People became increasingly aware of the exciting effects to be obtained by assembling a number of string players for the provision of dance music, and when the invention of opera in Italy in about 1600 resulted in public theatres springing up all over that country, orchestras became essential to fill these buildings with sound. The increasing use of Italian violins, violas, and violoncellos, with their brighter tones, also resulted in increased volume; consorts of viols had been effective enough in the halls of country houses, but for dance music they not only lacked volume but also rhythmic attack. The increasing popularity of ballet in larger and yet larger halls must have contributed considerably to the decline of the viol during the seventeenth century.

Louis XIV (1638-1715) was an early enthusiast for ballet. Himself a keen dancer, he grew up with a young Italian, Lully, who came to France at an early age and who was to prove one of the great composers of the seventeenth century. In most of the earlier ballet-style entertainments for which Lully wrote music, the king himself danced one of the leading parts. These entertainments were given in the palace hall in front of the king's friends, and the dancers wore costumes not very different from the normal 'party' dresses of the day. Not until the nineteenth century was there any serious attempt in European theatres to dress stage performers in historically accurate costumes, and at the court of Louis XIV gods and goddesses and other characters from mythology looked little different from lords and ladies. The long dresses that the ladies wore, and the heels on their shoes, made active dancing in the modern sense out of the question; dignity and a quiet, unathletic grace could be achieved, but not very much more.

The music for these entertainments usually included songs and choruses as well as dances, and these 'opera-ballets' were performed regularly in Paris for over a hundred years. Indeed, the tradition was so strong that until quite recent times it was obligatory for every opera given at the Paris Opera House to include a ballet. Even Verdi's *Otello*, first produced in 1887, could not be given there until the composer agreed to write some ballet music especially for this production (and very inappropriate it is!).

As Lully's opera-ballets became grander and grander the orchestra increased in size. Louis XIV's 'Twenty-four violins' are famous as being one of the earliest full-time orchestras (violas, cellos, and double-basses are included in the term 'violins'), and Lully himself ran an orchestra which was called 'Le petit Band'; it consisted of sixteen string players, and wind players as well. Oboes, bassoons, and trumpets would sometimes join the strings for special effects and occasionally the oboe players would play on recorder-type flutes. Much of the dance music was taken from the French countryside. Parisian courtiers enjoyed dressing up as peasants, and they can often be seen doing so in the paintings of Watteau. They would dance French country dances such as the minuet, the gavotte, and the bourrée, though, needless to say, their beautiful, gay, clean clothes bore as little relation to genuine peasant clothes as Lully's well-turned music bore to the rough bagpipe-and-drum effects that served to accompany genuine peasant dances. However, some suggestion of country rhythms and steps must have survived the sea-change that high society brought to them.

Here is a short gavotte which Lully wrote for the *Ballet des Plaisirs* (1655):

Another dance that Lully introduced into his ballets was the minuet, which was to become the rage of Europe.

Charles II had been much impressed with the 'Twenty-four violins' while in exile in Paris during the Cromwell régime, and he even went to the trouble of sending a young composer called Pelham Humfrey over to Paris to learn about their use. Unfortunately Humfrey died young, but everything French was so fashionable in London (then as now) that the rhythms of Lully's dances found their way not only into society balls but also on to the English stage; Purcell too wrote operas that included minuets and other dances, though not nearly so many as Lully's operas. In Germany and Austria the craze for the minuet was later to result in its regular inclusion in almost every type of instrumental work, from the keyboard suites of Bach to the symphonies of Haydn and Mozart.

Lully not only established Western European dance forms for a century and more; he also invented what is called the 'French overture,' and this too swept Europe. Its form was not invariable, but it usually began with a slow, stately introduction in dotted rhythm, followed by a quicker fugal movement; one or more short dances completed the overture. Bach's orchestral suites are, in effect, highly elaborate French overtures; the B minor has as many as six dances after the fugal movement. On the other hand, the overture to Handel's *Messiah* (also 'French') has no dances at all. Needless to say, overtures such as these were not intended for dancing; but their prototypes undoubtedly were. It has recently been suggested that Lully's slow introductions were written for the preliminary parade of dancers, rather like the parade that still takes place before a circus performance. If this is so, and it seems very likely, then these introductions are often played too slowly, for the four beats in each bar should clearly be in the time of four dignified steps. What happened during the subsequent fugue is less clear; fugues would not normally seem very well adjusted to the dance. Perhaps they represented an interlude after the parade during which the dancers collected themselves and prepared for the dances proper. These were usually short, the music being divided into two parts, each of which was played twice. (This is called 'binary' form.)

In England an entertainment that included singing, dancing, scenic effects, and some dialogue was called a masque. Masques had been especially popular at the English court at least as early as James I's reign, when the words were often written by Ben Jonson, and the music by composers who were either Italian (for instance, Alfonso Ferrabosco) or desirous of being thought Italian (for instance, John Cooper, who styled himself Giovanni Coperario). Unfortunately not very much of this music survives in full.

For many years after Lully's death ballet remained a constituent of opera: a large constituent in France and a small one in the other countries of Western Europe. Ladies' skirts became shorter, which made somewhat higher leg movements possible, but throughout the eighteenth century, owing to conventions of dress, male dancers still far outshone female dancers when agility was required.

The great contribution of the eighteenth century to ballet was the invention of the *ballet d'action*. In this the dancers not only aim to charm by the grace and agility of their movements; they also aim to tell a story in mime. The origin of the *ballet d'action* is extremely complicated and not fully understood, and it is only possible here to touch on a few aspects of a fascinating problem. The great French ballet-master, Noverre (1727-1810), is often credited with its invention, and certainly his *Lettres sur la Danse et sur les Ballets* and other writings suggest that he did more than anyone else to hasten its acceptance and, indeed, to establish the principles of modern ballet. But there had long been some small element of plot in the ballet, and pantomime was also showing the possibilities of comic, tragic, and sentimental miming. Noverre first came to London in 1755; Garrick called him "the Shakespeare of the Dance." Though he spent most of his time in Paris (Marie Antoinette was a pupil, and *Les Petits Riens*, for which Mozart wrote the music, was one of his ballets), he was in London fairly often, and during the Revolution he settled there for some years, after fleeing from Paris and leaving behind the savings of a lifetime.

As the story element is of such importance in the history of ballet let us glance at this aspect of certain works given in London in the latter half of the eighteenth century. First, a masque called *The Fairy Prince*, with music by Thomas Augustine Arne, the composer of *Rule, Britannia*. This must be one of the last examples of the masque in this country; it was produced at Covent Garden in 1771, near the end of Arne's career. About three-quarters of it consists of vocal music, and one-quarter of ballet music. Here is a list of the dances and their titles as given in the vocal score:

> *The Airs for the grand Dance of the Satyrs*
> *Gavotte: Figure Dance*
> *For the entrance of the Sylvans*
> *Chacoon*
> *The Sylvans make fresh Love to the Wood-Nymphs*
> *Here the Wood-Nymphs make returns of Love, and all dance in the following Movement*
> *The Fairies Country Dance, by the Children*
> *The first Grand March of the Procession* [trumpets only]
> *The second ditto* [also trumpets only]
> *Orchestra march*
> *When St George descends* [only five bars]
> *The first Air played at the Dinner*
> *The favourite Minuet play'd at the Dinner*

This is ballet much as Purcell would have understood it eighty years earlier, and Purcell would have liked much of the music, too, for some of it has a pleasantly English quality.

But clearly no one in the audience can have enjoyed these dances for their story interest; there was the merest apology for a plot. But the very next year Noverre was to produce what has been described as his first *ballet d'action* at the King's Theatre, in the Haymarket, in London, and though this had far less distinguished music, the ballet definitely aimed to tell a story. At the King's Theatre (where Italian operas were regularly given) ballets were not integrated into the operas as they were at Covent Garden and Drury Lane. They were given either between the acts of the operas or at the end, and had no connexion with the plot. The great music historian, Burney, records that the audience kept much quieter and paid more attention during the ballets than they did during the operas. Meanwhile, at Covent Garden and Drury Lane the Christmas pantomime was an annual event. These pantomimes were usually in two halves, of which the second was a traditional harlequinade deriving from the Italian *Commedia del arte*, and the first some new story; there was little connexion between the two. Occasionally there was some dialogue, and usually a song or two, but for the most part the effect depended on scenery and the miming of the performers to an appropriate orchestral accompaniment. Thus the very first pantomime ever to be based on the story of Robinson Crusoe appeared in 1781, with music by Thomas Linley. This music included one song, and sixty-four instrumental pieces, all very short and varying between eight and thirty bars in length. There is no dialogue. Here are the titles of the earlier pieces:

The Outside of Robinson Crusoe's Cave [oboe solo over pizzicato accompaniment]
Robinson Crusoe takes his gun
Parrot calls; Robinson Crusoe starts
Robinson Crusoe goes to work at the boat
Robinson Crusoe works on a tree
Robinson Crusoe sees the mark of a foot
March of Savages Landing
Dance of Savages

Here is the music of one of these pieces; it is not likely that the reader will guess which it is:

Though composers had been writing occasional pieces of descriptive music for at least two centuries, they seldom thought to do so in their theatre music; that was to come in the nineteenth century. But there is some attempt in *Robinson Crusoe* at matching the action in the music; for instance, when Crusoe discovers the footprint in the sand a sudden loud, quick ascending scale on the strings interrupts what was previously slow, peaceful music. Incidentally, this pantomime music is very like that which used to be played by pianists in the silent cinema; there is even one eighteenth-century pantomime with a piece called 'Hurry Music' in it.

Clearly the plot element was much stronger in the pantomime than in the masque. The characters were played partly by actors with a turn for dancing, and partly by dancers with a turn for burlesque and mime. Thus ballet and pantomime were coming closer together, and it was undoubtedly pantomime's proved ability to tell a story without words that made possible Noverre's emphasis on the story element. In 1785 Noverre even produced a ballet version of *Macbeth* without using words at all.

Whatever good Noverre did to the action of ballet, he did none at all to the music. It would be interesting to know more of his relations with composers. He nearly always chose nonentities to write his music, nonentities who would not have too many ideas of their own. The tradition he established of the third-rate composer and his complete subservience to the ballet-master (later to be called the choreographer) was to last nearly a century.

Further innovations followed after the turn of the century. When the girls lightened their clothes and got rid of their heels, and began (in the 1820's) experimenting with point work, the male dancer soon found himself eclipsed. The great vogue of the imported ballerina now began. Taglioni, Elssler, Grisi, and Cerrito brought a new spirit of ethereal beauty into ballet. Points gave the audience the sensation that the ballerina was almost taking flight, and it was not long before she did, aided by elaborate tackle, manipulated, out of sight, by sweating stage-hands. The Romantic ballet had arrived, with its emphasis on the female dancer and its relegation of the male to a purely subservient position as partner and lift-man. The poor composer was more subservient still and enjoyed no limelight whatever.

However, his music was stimulated to some extent by the dawn of the national dance. We have seen that French national dances had invigorated seventeenth-century ballet; the eighteenth century produced nothing new in this respect. It was the nineteenth century that saw the great reflowering of the national dance, and it was the dances from Eastern Europe that were to make the most vigorous impression. Romantic ballet was just too early to profit from these, but at least the Viennese waltz arrived in time. The waltz was to the nineteenth century what the minuet had been to the eighteenth. It is said to have developed from the German peasant dance known as the *Ländler*, and by the 1830's Vienna (and, for that matter, the rest of Europe) was waltz-mad.

And so we arrive at the year 1841, when *Giselle* first saw the light of day. Ballet music had progressed some way since Linley's *Robinson Crusoe*. After 1800 dances became longer and were often linked together, so that the music flowed more continuously. Also, composers were making attempts, if only rudimentary ones, to catch the mood of the situation in their music; in other words, they no longer left all the drama to the miming. We shall find that from now on the orchestra plays an ever-increasing part in conveying the plot, in setting the scene, in creating dramatic tension, and in characterizing the chief personages.

Chapter Three
ADAM AND THE ROMANTIC BALLET
Giselle

Score. No published full score or orchestral parts seem to exist, and there are as many versions of the music, as regards both substance and scoring, as there are companies performing the work. The following versions are worth mentioning:

1. The piano arrangement published in 1841 by Meissonier in Paris, and reissued later, using the same plates, by H. le Boulch. This is not now obtainable new, but it is by no means a rare publication. *It is the only published version of " Giselle " with any claim to authenticity.*
2. The piano arrangement published in 1924 by Max Eschig; it represents Henri Busser's version as then used at the Paris Opéra. It is the only version of *Giselle* now obtainable new (from Schott) but differs widely from both 1. and 3.
3. The Covent Garden version, a manuscript score to which both Gordon Jacob and Robert Irving have made contributions; incredibly, no one now remembers who orchestrated the greater part of it. It was not Adam. At the end of this chapter there is an appendix showing the extent to which 1. and 3. differ, and it will be seen that Covent Garden make innumerable cuts, both large and small, shortening the ballet by nearly half an hour. To offset these there are additions to the original, of which much the most considerable is the long *pas de deux* for two peasants in Act I. Here Covent Garden employ music by Burgmüller, orchestrated by Robert Irving (Burgmüller was a German composer, admired by Schumann, who died young in 1836); but this was a common addition to the ballet in an inferior orchestration before Irving's day, and is danced also by the Royal Swedish Ballet. The cuts date mostly from before the War and were made by Sergeiev and Constant Lambert, but performances in Britain in 1956 by the Bolshoi Ballet and in 1957 by the Royal Swedish Ballet revealed that there is everything to be said for restoring the cuts, and Covent Garden may soon stage a fuller version, musically much closer to the original. It is hoped too that the original orchestration will be restored. This should soon be possible, as Adam's original score has recently come to light in America.

Recordings.[1] H.M.V. DLP 1004 has ten numbers only, played by the Covent Garden Orchestra under Robert

[1] The Appendix gives full details of all recordings mentioned in the book.

Irving, and does not aim at continuity. Decca LXT 2844 contains the Busser version, much cut, and with some additions peculiar to itself.

Giselle is commonly said to be the earliest ballet of which the choreography is still remembered, and though in fact by no means all of it is remembered (for much of the original music has fallen out of use and been in part replaced by fresh music with new choreography), in Paris, at least, the ballet has never dropped out of the repertoire for longer than the span of a ballet-master's memory. No one would dare to wipe the slate clean and devise entirely new steps to the music. On the other hand, few dancers have hesitated to make additions, with choreography of their own devising, to music that Adam would not have owned. Some of these, as we shall see, have become hallowed by time and are now accepted as part of the work by many companies. Others have been regarded by individual dancers as their own property, the music jealously guarded for fear some rival company should steal the dance. It is often hard to tell if the origin of a piece of ballet music is unrecorded through mere indifference or as a matter of policy.

Giselle was first performed on June 28, 1841, in Paris. The choreographer was Jean Coralli, and the story is ascribed to Théophile Gautier, who is said to have adapted an idea of Heine's. *Giselle* survives because it combines all that was best in the Romantic ballet. The story breathes the very essence of Romanticism. The music, though far from great, is wonderfully effective in its place, and decidedly better than most ballet music of its day. Above all, the story is ingeniously devised to tax the full range of the ballerina's art. In the first act she must charm with simple innocence and later, when she goes mad, horrify by sheer dramatic power: in the second act, when she joins the ghosts of other disappointed lovers, her dancing must have an other-worldliness, a mystical, floating quality. In fact, Giselle is a whale of a part, the ballerina's Hamlet, and very few dancers are equally successful in both acts. Carlotta Grisi, who created the rôle in 1841 and danced it in London the following year, is said to have been unequalled in the ethereal second act. But when Fanny Elssler took up the part and brought a new sense of drama to the mad scene Grisi, aware of her limitations, never danced the first act again and would only give the second. During the first few decades of its existence it was surprisingly rare for this ballet to be given complete. In our own time the Giselles of both Alicia Markova and Margot Fonteyn have been among the few glories of the London stage.

The ingredients of *Giselle* were not especially new. Mad scenes were a commonplace in opera—for instance, in Donizetti's *Lucia di Lammermoor*, produced in 1835. Furthermore, sylphs, both dead and alive, and many of them airborne, were frequently to be seen on the stages of Europe—for instance, in *La Sylphide*, which the great Taglioni had danced in London in 1832. The heroine falls in love with a Scotsman, a circumstance hard to parallel in the ballet world. The music survives in piano score, but is without merit, while the choreography is lost, though there have been several attempts to invent new steps to the music. *Giselle* outlasted *La Sylphide* because of the oneness of its action and music, and because of their very real quality.

Adolphe Adam (1803-56), who wrote the music for *Giselle*, must have expected to be remembered for his light operas, which were numerous; he did not often descend to ballet. Played on the piano, much of *Giselle* sounds thin and feeble; so, for that matter, do Italian operas of this time—for instance, Donizetti's and Verdi's (in his early days). One has to go to the theatre to discover that these composers were highly competent professionals whose music, though ineffective on the modern piano (for which it was not intended), is nevertheless exactly calculated to delight a theatre audience when danced or sung. Apart from some pretty tunes, *Giselle* contains a number of original touches, in particular, an incipient leitmotiv system and an early example of the dramatic use of musical reminiscence. Unfortunately, ballet companies do all they can to conceal Adam's leitmotivs; the tune associated with Hilarion is either cut out entirely or halved each time it appears. The best

Giselle and Albrecht

of the 'fear' themes associated with the Wilis is not to be heard at Covent Garden. Of the more obvious leitmotivs only that for the peasants (A) remains prominent. Nevertheless, Adam deserves credit for the device, and many subsequent composers of ballet music copied him in this respect.

Giselle is in two acts; it lasts rather less than an hour and a half and was never intended to provide a full evening's entertainment on its own. A large proportion of the first act is mimed rather than danced.

ACT I

The scene is "near the Rhine." After a brief introduction we see a glade in a forest, with small cottages to left and right; in the distance there is a castle. We catch a glimpse of Loys, the hero, going into the cottage on the right; the gamekeeper, Hilarion, also appears for a moment, but almost at once a crowd of villagers fills the stage.

When they have gone Loys meets Wilfred, who is grandly dressed, and we discover from their miming that the plain peasant clothes that Loys is wearing are a disguise; he is really a count and Wilfred is his attendant. The reason for his disguise lives in the left-hand cottage: the beautiful but lowly born Giselle. With jealous eyes Hilarion sees Count Albrecht (as we must now call him) knocking on Giselle's door. (Hilarion himself has been jilted by Giselle, presumably displaced by the handsome stranger.) Giselle appears from the cottage without a care in the world.

In the *Scène d'Amour* the lovers flirt innocently to sadly sweet music.

Giselle picks the petals off a flower, but "he loves me not" is the ominous result. This scene is mimed, not danced. Hilarion emerges from his hiding-place and threatens Albrecht, but a crowd of girls, carrying the grape harvest in baskets, interrupt the quarrel (A), and soon Giselle joins them in a waltz.

At this point a *pas de deux* for Giselle and Albrecht is usually inserted; the original piano version puts it much later in the act.

This dance is interrupted by the entrance of Giselle's mother, Berthe, who remonstrates with her daughter for over-taxing her strength by too much dancing.

Giselle pleads to be allowed to go on (a snatch of D), but this is forbidden. If her exertions prove fatal Giselle may become a Wili; at this warning Berthe's tune contracts its intervals menacingly (F2). (The Wilis were betrothed girls who had died before their wedding-day and, unable to rest quietly in their graves, danced endlessly as shades.)

The stage is cleared, and Hilarion furtively ventures into Albrecht's cottage.

(This is Hilarion's leitmotiv; we should also have heard it soon after the curtain went up, but it is usually cut at this point.) Hunting horns announce that the local Duke and his daughter, the Princess, are approaching.

Tired from the chase, they have come for refreshment and rest. Tables and chairs are set out, and Giselle provides drinks for the hunting party.

Giselle is overcome with admiration for the Princess's beautiful clothes, while the Princess, on her side, is impressed by Giselle's beauty and inquires in mime what she does with herself. Giselle replies that she works as a peasant by day (A) and dances in the evening, and she coyly shows off a snatch of the waltz (D) until her mother stops her (F). At this point Covent Garden inserts a long *pas de deux*, danced by two peasants for the entertainment of the gentry. The royal party then retires into Giselle's cottage for rest. From the other cottage comes Hilarion (G) gloating over a great sword he has found there, a magnificently crested sword which could not possibly belong to a peasant. He hides it in a bush and waits for a suitable moment to make his revelation. Then follows the so-called *March of the Vineyard Workers*, a quick piece in six-eight time that calls for dancing rather than marching. Albrecht, who has had his own reasons for keeping out of the way while the hunting party was about, now returns (and it is at this point that the *pas de deux* (E) *should* be danced, Giselle's mother having rather weakly given way to her daughter's plea). At Covent Garden Giselle dances a variation[1] to a tune which Adam would not have recognized; *importée des Ballets Russes*, according to the Busser score:

In the galop that follows all join in.

Hilarion now feels that his time has come. He strides to the middle of the crowded stage, the great sword in his hand, and points accusingly at Albrecht, the owner of the sword—

---

[1] A variation is a short solo dance. It has no connexion with the 'variations on a theme' to be found in instrumental music.

no peasant, but a nobleman in disguise, an impostor. In fury, Albrecht flings himself on Hilarion.

They are separated. Giselle watches, stupefied, while Hilarion blows on his hunting horn to summon the royal party from the cottage. All is revealed; Albrecht is not only a nobleman, but betrothed to the Princess. Giselle, realizing that all her hopes of him are shattered, slumps on to the ground, and it is at this point, with the music suddenly hushed after the tragic excitement of L, that the famous mad scene begins. To the music of the *Scène d'Amour* (C) Giselle slowly rises from the ground, and it is clear that her senses have left her. She recalls pathetically the petals she pulled from the flower, and, coming on the sword which has been left where it fell in the scuffle, she seizes it and to every one's horror begins dancing to snatches of the *pas de deux* (E). Not until it is too late, and she has run the sword through herself, can any of the hypnotized onlookers stir. Albrecht's tragic despair (L) is of no avail.

Act II

The scene changes to another part of the wood, at night, with Giselle's newly dug grave dimly seen in the background; there is a cross above it. There should be a long scene at the start for Hilarion, horrified at the result of his jealousy. The music recalls A and H as he warns some huntsmen that the place is haunted, and E as he remembers how beautifully Giselle danced. All this is cut at Covent Garden, which begins with the music depicting midnight striking and with only the briefest glimpse of Hilarion. (The Decca recording begins Act II with some highly impressionistic music utterly out of keeping with Adam's style: its source is not known to me.) When Hilarion has gone Myrtha, Queen of the Wilis, appears and dances with slow, ethereal steps in the moonlight.

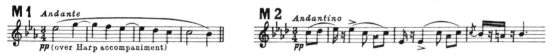

The music of her second tune is perhaps less in keeping with the situation than the first. Soon the other Wilis are dancing with her.

To quiet, almost mysterious music, Giselle rises from her grave.

She is accepted as a new member of this shadowy troupe. When, eventually, the glade is left empty Albrecht stumbles in with Wilfred; the music expresses his misery.

Wilfred pleads with Albrecht to come home, but Albrecht insists on staying to mourn for his beloved and dismisses his attendant. He is in great danger, for mortals who encounter Wilis by night are driven mad. Suddenly the shade of Giselle flits past him; and then again and again. (In 1841 she was airborne on wires.) She at least cannot but be loving still. They dance a dreamlike, insubstantial *pas de deux* together.

Albrecht hides when the Wilis return. Coming on the luckless Hilarion, they drive him out of his senses and hound him into the nearby lake. They would do the same to Albrecht, whom they find soon after, and in the original ballet, to the music of an interesting and wholly unexpected fugue, the Wilis—the powers of evil—are foiled by Giselle's holding a cross in her hand. Myrtha orders that Albrecht must dance till he drops, and his long *pas de deux* with Giselle is watched by all the Wilis, as it were waiting for the kill.

As other tunes follow, their desperate pleadings to be allowed to stop this dance of death are refused by Myrtha. At Covent Garden Giselle has a variation (C changed into waltz rhythm) which is given in the Busser score but not in the original; Busser did not know who wrote it. Albrecht, sustained by Giselle's love, lasts out until the first grey light of dawn dispels the Wilis. Giselle sinks back into her grave, and Wilfred finds Albrecht lying alone and exhausted in the glade.

Musically, the second act of Giselle is less successful than the first. It was not within Adam's powers to devise sufficiently ethereal music for these after-death situations, though it must be remembered that we, with our knowledge of the half-lights obtained by composers such as Debussy, cannot judge the effect of this music on Adam's contemporaries. Almost certainly it seemed more ethereal to them than it ever can to us. But the finale of the first act is a masterpiece judged by any standards applicable to ballet. The device of repeating tunes first heard in happy circumstances—of repeating them reminiscently when all hope is gone—is extraordinarily effective. The contrast between the tragedy of the situation and the happiness of the music poignantly suggests what might have been. In Gounod's *Faust* it is one of the waltz themes that is recalled in this manner, while the most pathetic example known to me comes at the end of Puccini's *La Bohème*, when Mimi, on her deathbed but reunited with Rudolph, calls to mind some of their love duet in the first act. These operas are later than *Giselle*, but the device can be found in rudimentary form in earlier operas, such as Donizetti's *Lucia di Lammermoor* (1835) and Bellini's *La Sonnambula* (1831). As already mentioned, *Lucia* also has a mad scene, and here too the heroine recalls a snatch of the love scene from an earlier act. But Adam's more fragmentary reminiscences seem to me more dramatically ingenious and effective. Of all the ballets discussed in this book *Giselle* has, let us admit it, the least interesting music for the armchair listener. But it is by no means the least effective in the theatre, and musicians will probably feel more favourably disposed towards it when the cuts are restored—for instance, the fugue, which comes off splendidly and is even graced with the scholastic device known as augmentation.[1] It is significant that there should be a fugue at all, for in general Adam disapproved of them

---

1 When the theme appears in notes of double length.

in stage works. In his *Derniers Souvenirs d'un Musicien* he wrote, "Many should be written in class to acquire the art of distributing the parts, but as few as possible in practice, and least of all for the stage, where their use is to be justified only by a wholly exceptional situation." Clearly he felt that the clash of good and evil in Act II of *Giselle* was a wholly exceptional situation.

Cuts and Alterations made in the Covent Garden Production

I have compiled this list for the benefit of those who have access to one of the early piano arrangements; the references are to the old piano score (1. above).

ACT I

Introduction. Bars 4-7 cut. Curtain is up for the andante, during which Hilarion sees Albrecht go into his cottage.

No. 1. P. 4, bar 35, to p. 5, bar 41 cut.

No. 2. P. 7, bars 6-18 cut.

No. 3. P. 13, bars 8-23 cut.

No. 4. P. 14, bars 20½-32½ cut.

P. 19. After last bar, insert piece in A flat from p. 39 to p. 41.

P. 21, bars 4-13 and 16-21 cut; also first four bars of bottom line.

No. 5. P. 22. Cut whole page except last two bars.

P. 23, bars 9-29 cut.

P. 28, bar 22, to p. 29, bar 16 cut.

P. 30. Music on this page much shortened. Long *pas de deux* inserted at end of No. 5.

No. 6. P. 31, bar 17, to end cut.

P. 34, line 2, to end of p. 41 all cut and replaced by variation for Giselle given in Busser score (*not* by Adam).

No. 8. P. 46. From bar 3 onward every other bar is cut; in bars 15-22 alternate pairs of bars are cut.

ACT II

No. 9. Pp. 56-59 cut.

P. 60. Line 3 to bar 1 of p. 61 cut.

No. 10. P. 63, bar 23, to p. 64, bar 6 cut; also whole of E flat section (pp. 64-65).

No. 12. P. 76. First 14 bars in F; then cut to end of line 2 on p. 79.

No. 13. P. 80. Bars 1-13 cut.

P. 81. Cut 9 bars from *animato*.

P. 85. Cut from *plus lent* to end of page, then insert apocryphal variation for Giselle (not in Busser; apparently only danced by Markova).

No. 14. P. 92. Line 4 is altered harmonically and leads straight into No. 15, cutting the fugue.

No. 15. P. 98. At double bar in last line waltz version of the *Scène d'Amour* is inserted; this is given by Busser. It is certainly not by Adam.

One final word about the two apocryphal dances given in the Busser piano arrangement and danced at Covent Garden: Giselle's variation in Act I (K) and the waltz version of C to which she dances in Act II. In each case Busser provides a footnote stating that their authorship is unknown and that both were introduced by the Russian Ballet. This edition came out in·1924, and before then the only performances of *Giselle* in Western Europe by the Russian Ballet had been the somewhat unsuccessful ones given by the Diaghilev company in 1910. Did Tcherepnin perhaps compose these two numbers? More probably they were written for one of Petipa's productions in Russia twenty or thirty years earlier, by Minkus or Drdla, and automatically adopted by the Diaghilev company.

Chapter Four

DELIBES AND THE FRENCH BALLET

Coppélia   Sylvia

Léo Delibes (1836-91) shared with John Dunstable and Boito the distinction of being left out of the first edition of *Grove's Dictionary of Music and Musicians*—which is not very surprising, as in 1889 scarcely anyone in England would have heard of him. His ballets took a long time to reach this country; *Coppélia* was not given here until 1906, and *Sylvia*, presented in a potted one-act version in 1911, does not seem to have been staged complete until the Covent Garden production in 1952. The fact is that scarcely any long ballets were allowed on to the London stage before the First World War, it being supposed impossible for people's attention to be held by a whole evening of dancing. Tchaikovsky's also had to wait until long after the composer's death. Those of Delibes had the added disadvantage, as has already been noted, that no full scores of them were obtainable. Yet the orchestral suites from *Coppélia* and *Sylvia* must be counted among the most frequently played light music of the nineteenth century.

Delibes was a pupil of Adam, the composer of *Giselle*, but far excelled his master as a composer. His orchestration has gusto, clarity, and often considerable originality, his tunes have charm, and, above all, his music at its best has a 'lift' that makes it eminently suitable for dancing. To hear the mazurka from *Coppélia* for the first time is an enviable experience. In later life Delibes turned to opera, where he was not always successful at tuning music to the deeper emotions, but in *Coppélia* and *Sylvia* he achieved something not far short of perfection. He is a much underrated composer.

As is often stated, Delibes was the first nineteenth-century composer of real distinction to write ballet music, and for this reason his importance historically is tremendous. But it should be added that he was not asked to write *Coppélia* because he was considered a great composer; he was asked because he was just one of several promising young hacks willing to produce what was required of them. It was pure chance that he turned out to be not a hack composer at all.

In form, his ballets scarcely differ from *Giselle*. There are far more national dances, mostly for the *corps de ballet* (for nationalism in music was the latest craze), but no suites of dances of the kind that were to form so important a part of the later 'classical' ballets of Tchaikovsky. Like Adam, Delibes had a fondness for associating themes with characters; but no great respect is shown for his intentions nowadays—at least, as regards *Coppélia*. There is a complication here; though the ballet was originally performed with choreography by Arthur Saint-Léon, it is usually given in this country with choreography by Lev Ivanov, the choreographer who worked with Petipa on the Tchaikovsky ballets in the 1890's. How far Ivanov preserved Saint-Léon's ideas I do not know, but wherever the choreography seems to be at variance with the music it seems reasonable to lay the blame on Ivanov. With *Sylvia* there is no dead-wood tradition; indeed, there is no tradition at all, for no one pretends to know what was done in the original production. Those who have recreated the ballet in recent times must have been grateful for the detailed account of the action printed above the music in the published piano arrangement.

Coppélia

Score. No full score or parts have ever been published. Until recently Covent Garden and Sadler's Wells used a manuscript score of which the third act was orchestrated by Gordon Jacob, but now all three acts are played in the original orchestration. The original piano arrangement, which has copious stage directions can be obtained from United Music Publishers.

Recordings. H.M.V. CLP 1046 contains about half the ballet, Decca LXT 5342-43 the whole of it.

Coppélia was first given in Paris in 1870; the plot was based on a story called *Der Sandmann*, by E. T. A. Hoffmann, later used for Act I of Offenbach's *The Tales of Hoffmann*. The choreography was by Saint-Léon. Its success was cut short by the outbreak of the Franco-Prussian War after the eighteenth performance; the sixteen-year-old Italian girl who created the heroine, Swanilda, died during the siege of Paris.

The part of the hero, Frantz, was originally taken by a girl; it was a *travesty* part—that is, one in which the sexes are reversed—and this arrangement affected the structure of the ballet. There is no *pas de deux* for Frantz and Swanilda (though one is engineered during the last act in all modern productions), and Frantz has very little dancing to do of any kind. He has, however, a great deal of miming, and Delibes has established him dramatically with two leitmotivs. With great ingenuity the recording companies have managed to omit the first of these from all discs of this ballet, except in the recent complete version, despite the fact that it occurs a great many times. It is perhaps better suited to a girl impersonating a man than to the male dancer of modern productions:

Frantz's other leitmotiv suggests him in more sentimental vein.

It will be noticed that the first four notes of these two tunes are alike. Frantz spends most of the ballet in love with a doll, Coppélia, under the misapprehension that she is real. Coppélia is excellently characterized in a stiff little canon.

Dotted rhythms and dry canonic devices are also associated with Coppélia's creator, a formidable old gentleman called Dr Coppélius.

Act I

The Prelude consists of a slow introduction followed by a mazurka; all the tunes recur later in the ballet. (This is not the case with the *Giselle* Prelude.) The slow introduction is taken note for note, but with changed orchestration, from the incident in Act II when Dr Coppélius is trying by his magic powers to transfer Frantz's soul to the doll he has made, Frantz at the time being drugged and asleep. The first tune beautifully expresses this situation.

Swanilda watches as Frantz makes Advances to Coppélia

This leads into a version of B, Frantz's tune, but lifted above the ordinary by an alteration to its last note; this is raised a semitone, and the modulation this heralds breathes magic into the music. Then follows a shortened version of the famous mazurka.

The curtain goes up on the square of a little town. The fresh, vernal phrases for unaccompanied clarinet, oboe, and flute were written to accompany the heroine, Swanilda, as she comes from her house and greets the morning; they make an incongruous accompaniment for the mysterious Dr Coppélius, whom we see going into his house in some modern productions at this point. The first music of any substance is Swanilda's waltz.

Alone in the square, Swanilda gazes curiously at Dr Coppélius's house—more particularly at its balcony, on which there is a girl sitting reading a book. The girl keeps very still, and takes no notice of Swanilda's attempts to attract her attention. At the end of the waltz Swanilda sees Frantz coming and hides. Frantz is her fiancé, and her suspicions of his infidelity are confirmed by his behaviour in the square. He too tries to attract the mysterious girl's attention (A). Strange rumblings are heard from Dr Coppélius's house, and to stiff, mechanical music (C) the girl, Coppélia, starts moving her head and arms in a stiff, mechanical way. Frantz blows her a kiss. Swanilda comes from her hiding-place and reproaches him, and he rather unconvincingly protests that he still loves her (B; also A). Townspeople swarm into the square and dance the mazurka (E). When it is over the Burgomaster announces that there is to be a holiday the following day to celebrate the Duke's gift of a bell to the town, and that all who are married on this day will be given a dowry by the Duke. He is interrupted by more strange rumblings from Dr Coppélius's house; to a perky little tune on the violins Swanilda reassures the somewhat startled townsfolk. To the music of the *Ballade* (G), the Burgomaster asks Swanilda if she and Frantz are to be married, and she tests his faithfulness with an ear of corn.

None of her friends can hear anything when she holds the corn to their ears, and this means that her hopes are gone; she runs off in tears. She soon returns, however, to join her six girl friends in the *Thème Slave Varié*; here is the theme (taken from a work by the Polish composer, Moniuszko):

This has five variations (in the musical sense):

Variation 1. Tune alternates between clarinets and oboes, with violin decorations here and there. Danced by Swanilda's six friends.

Variation 2. Tune on the cellos, with oboes and horns taking a hand in it later; rapid scales above on the violins. Also danced by the six friends.

Variation 3. Tune in new rhythm alternately loud (for full orchestra) and soft (for woodwind). A solo for Swanilda.

Variation 4. A clarinet solo. The six friends begin it, and Swanilda joins in in the middle. After an interlude of trills, during which Swanilda bows, and her friends imitate her, there is a final quick, extended variation.

There follows a Hungarian czardas for all the townsfolk, at first slow and then suddenly wild.

This is followed by a *sortie*,[1] based on a phrase from the quick section of the czardas, followed by some ruminating on the first half-bar of J. (Is it a coincidence that J and K start in rather a similar way?) By the time the music has quietened down the square is empty.

To stiff, dry music, old Dr Coppélius comes from his house, his pedagogy suggested by canonic device.

Jostled by some youths, he drops his door-key and, unaware of this catastrophe, makes his way out of the square. Swanilda, passing by with her girl friends, finds it, and curiosity overcomes her; the orchestra plays C to let us know the object of her curiosity. They all creep into the mysterious house, a little giggly and aware that they are doing wrong. No sooner have they disappeared than Frantz comes furtively into the square, carrying a ladder (A). He has momentary qualms about Swanilda (B), but the thought of Coppélia (C) spurs him on to prop the ladder up against her balcony. The return of Dr Coppélius, searching for his key, frightens him away. Dr Coppélius hurries into his house. (In some modern productions Frantz returns and is seen climbing the ladder as the curtain falls.)

ACT II

Act II may be supposed to start before the end of Act I—that is, as the girls go into the house. After a brief *entr'acte*, characterized by Dr Coppélius's stiff, dotted rhythms, together with a reminder of Swanilda's waltz, we find ourselves in the old gentleman's sanctum on the first floor. The music suggests the girls tiptoeing in.

[1] A short piece of music to get people off the stage.

Dr Coppélius surprises Swanilda and her Friends in his Workshop

Swanilda is the first to appear, rather frightened; her friends do not venture in until the repeat of the main tune. It is a strange room, full of life-size figures—dolls, presumably; or are they alive? Swanilda draws the window curtains, and there at the back on the balcony is Coppélia, still reading (C). Swanilda greets her and gets no answer. The girls crowd round, and at last Swanilda ventures to touch her. Coppélia too is a doll! They are all delighted with this discovery, and the orchestra plays B while they relish the fact that Frantz is in love with a puppet. Soon they have all the dolls in the room wound up and displaying their mechanical tricks to some ingenious mechanical music.

But retribution is at hand—they are, after all, behaving very badly—and, to their dismay, Dr Coppélius comes storming in. He stops the automata, draws the curtain to conceal Coppélia, and chases the girls out of his house. He is not aware that one of them, Swanilda, is still behind the curtain. Thinking that all is well, and that no damage has been done, he breathes a sigh of relief. And then he sees the unlucky Frantz at the top of his ladder (A) and catches him. However, his fury soon gives way to cunning. "I'm not as bad as you think," he seems to say, and he fetches some wine. Frantz imprudently drinks some, to a suspiciously innocent little tune.

Soon he is slumped over the table, quite insensible. Dr Coppélius is delighted; this is the chance for which he has long hoped. His masterpiece, Coppélia, has everything but a soul. Can he transfer Frantz's soul to Coppélia by magic powers? (C recurs at this point.) Dr Coppélius consults some very learned-looking books, and as he wheels his puppet in her chair from behind the curtain into the room, and attempts a spell, we hear the music (A) that comes at the very start of the ballet (but this time high on muted violins, and sounding like the beginning of *Lohengrin*), followed by C. The 'puppet' blinks her eyes.

Has the spell worked? She makes stiff little movements with her arms and head, and even her feet, movements far too elaborate for a doll. The old gentleman's joy knows no bounds when she breaks into a stiff little waltz.

But she still does not move naturally; he is still not satisfied that she has a soul. After more turning of musty pages—a calm, lovely oboe solo—success seems to be his at last.

By this time even the youngest member of the audience is aware that this is not Coppélia at all; Swanilda has taken her place, having put on her clothes while hidden behind the curtain. She is now playing up to the good doctor for all she is worth and thoroughly enjoying herself. Her movements get more and more natural—almost too much so, as far as he is concerned: he is only just in time to stop her drinking some of Frantz's drugged wine (N). Wandering round the room, she comes on Frantz (A). What is this? "Just an automaton like the others," says Dr Coppélius mendaciously. She picks up a sword and amuses herself by chasing the doctor round the room; then she turns flirtatious and entertains the old gentleman with a couple of sprightly national dances, the first a Spanish bolero.

(During the first part she is putting on a Spanish mantilla; usually she only starts to dance when the music goes into the major.) The second is a Scottish jig, and here too some suitable fancy-dressing takes place.

By this time Dr Coppélius scarcely knows where he is. The act ends with a spirited fugue (did Adam teach Delibes to put fugues in his ballets?).

Frantz wakes up, takes in the situation, and, with Swanilda, rushes round setting all the automata in motion, including Coppélia herself (C). Dr Coppélius realizes he has been made a fool of, and by the time the two young people have escaped down the ladder his room has become a shambles.

ACT III

This is the most plotless act in any ballet which tells a story. After the ceremony of giving the bell a number of couples are married, including Frantz and Swanilda, and then the stage is given over to a *divertissement*, during which much of the original choreography is ignored, judging by the evidence of the piano arrangement, no two companies diverging in the same way. Here is a list of the dances as given in the piano score:

Marche de la Cloche
Divertissement
    1. *Valse des Heures*
    2. *L'Aurore*
    3. *La Prière*
    4. *Le Travail (La Fileuse)*
    5. *L'Hymen*
    6. *La Discorde et la Guerre*
    7. *La Paix*
       Danse de Fête
    8. *Galop Final*

Little notice is taken of the titles in any choreography known to me, and usually the order is changed. Both the Royal Ballet companies use *La Paix* as a *pas de deux* for Frantz and Swanilda and follow it with a variation for Swanilda (*Le Travail*) and one for Frantz (part of *Discorde et la Guerre*). Until recently some music from near the end of *Sylvia* was used for Frantz's solo, and the rather unpleasant *Discorde et la Guerre* was cut altogether. There is some fine music in this act, but its dramatic impact is nil.

There is no other ballet heroine mentioned in this book who is in the least like Swanilda. She is neither ethereal nor spiritual, and, unlike Giselle, Odette, Aurora, and all the rest of them, she has a sense of humour. She is in fact a good deal more human than ballet heroines commonly are, and also more individual, with her self-assurance and courage. Swanilda is what might be called a soubrette part—a gay, almost pert creature, not waiting to be courted but dominating the action of the story. The success of the ballet depends first and foremost on the fact that Delibes has managed to match his heroine with gay, almost pert music exactly fitted to the action; his dramatic instincts are extraordinarily sound. One must also add that the story is of unusual interest, and that the national dances are extremely vivid. There is a great deal of miming in this ballet, and Delibes must have welcomed the national dance convention as an excuse to work some pure dancing into the action. The action of *Coppélia* is supposed to take place on the borders of Galicia, in southern Poland, not far from the Hungarian border (or rather, what was the Hungarian border in those days). Thus it is by no means incongruous that the townspeople should dance a mazurka and a czardas. There are a good many Hungarian touches in the score; for instance, the ballade (G) contains the commonest of all Hungarian gipsy cadences:

Delibes no doubt got his knowledge of such things from Liszt's Hungarian Rhapsodies. The *Coppélia* example is said to be the first czardas in theatre music. It was certainly not the last. Tchaikovsky, who was much influenced by Delibes and took over his national dance idea lock, stock, and barrel, has a similar czardas in *Swan Lake*, written some five years later.

For extra local colour Delibes borrowed a tune from the Polish composer Moniuszko (1819–72), whose national opera *Halka* (1854) has always been regarded by Poles as one of the great patriotic gestures of the nineteenth century. It is odd that the origin of this

tune—the *Thème Slave*—is not given in early editions of *Coppélia*. One wonders if some legal action was threatened. The piano scores that can be bought to-day differ from those of 1870 only in the fact that this tune is now attributed to Moniuszko's *Échos de Pologne*. This is a book of songs and duets, many of them in mazurka rhythm, which was published in Paris in 1865 with French words. Whether there was ever a version with Polish words I do not know. The theme which attracted the attention of Delibes is a duet, and it is headed *Cracoviak*—a dance supposed to have originated in Cracow, and thus in the area where the story of *Coppélia* is laid. Delibes has altered the tune slightly and improved the accompaniment, which is extremely unenterprising in the original. I have given it opposite in a slightly simplified form to save space, with the two vocal lines in the treble clef; I have omitted four bars of semi-quaver triplet octaves for the piano at the start. It makes an attractive song.

Sylvia

Score. No published full score seems to exist. Many of the linking passages to be heard at Covent Garden, and no doubt some of the dances, have been orchestrated from the piano score by Robert Irving. This piano score is a good one, containing much information about the action; in many passages it indicates which instrument is playing the tune. It can be bought from United Music Publishers.
Recording. H.M.V. CLP 1058, played by the Covent Garden Orchestra under Robert Irving, contains a good half of the music. A vertical line in the margin of the following synopsis indicates which passages are covered on this record.

Sylvia, ou la Nymphe de Diane was first produced in Paris in 1876. The story was taken from Tasso's pastoral drama, *Aminta*, by Jules Barbier (who also had a hand in Gounod's *Faust*) and Baron de Reinach, and the choreography (now long forgotten) was by Louis Mérante. It is a full-length ballet, and the last that Delibes wrote; thereafter he turned his attention to opera. As has been stated earlier, *Sylvia* was not given complete in Britain until Covent Garden put it on in 1952 with new choreography by Frederick Ashton. The plot was far from original; ballets about nymphs and goddesses had been a commonplace almost since the days of Louis XIV and earlier. But the music was highly original; its almost symphonic dimensions, ingenious orchestration, and sense of style set new standards.

Like *Coppélia*, *Sylvia* has a fairly elaborate leitmotiv system, though once again there is no theme for the all-important heroine.

Aminta, the hero, who is a shepherd, has a cool Attic melody usually heard on the flute (A1); it might almost have been written by Ravel. The amorous side of his nature is shown in a wide-ranging cello tune (A2).

Orion, the villain, has no more than a phrase.

The Cortège Rustique

Eros (L'Amour) understandably has a warmer, more lyrical tune.

Though there is no theme for Sylvia, there are a great many horn calls in the ballet, due to the importance to the plot of the huntress nymphs of Diana, of whom Sylvia is one.

ACT I

The Prelude is a somewhat carelessly constructed piece that begins and ends with a tune from the *Cortège de Bacchus* in Act III (L). In between, in quick succession, come some quiet horn calls,

also a tune for clarinet, heard later when Sylvia pulls the arrow from Aminta's body, Orion's menacing little phrase (B), and, rather incongruously, the greater part of the *Cortège Rustique* from near the end of Act I.

The curtain goes up on a sacred wood in the moonlight; at the back is a small temple and in front of it a statue of Eros. Fauns and Dryads are disporting themselves to one of Delibes' lithe, wide-ranging tunes.

When their games take them in mock supplication to the statue of Eros we hear C. The arrival of the shepherd Aminta (A1) sends them scurrying away. He has come in search of Sylvia; his one previous glimpse of her had an overwhelming effect on his desires (A2). He hides as horn calls (D) herald her arrival with the other huntresses, and they dance in honour of the chase; this is the piece known as *Les Chasseresses*.

It will be noticed that this tune derives from the second of the horn calls (D2, the bracketed portion). There follows the equally famous *Intermezzo* (both pieces are in the well-known concert suite); it is danced by Sylvia.

Towards the end of this dance an evil figure appears behind some rocks: it is Orion, *le chasseur noir, la terreur des forêts*. He too watches Sylvia with amorous eyes. Some of the nymphs come on Aminta's cloak and drag him from his hiding-place; Sylvia is horrified that he should dare to love an immortal (A1), but Aminta points to Eros as the cause (A2). Sylvia, indignant, shoots an arrow at the statue, but Aminta, to protect the love-god, puts himself in the way and the arrow pierces his chest; he falls. Sylvia is not in the least sorry for him and curses Eros. As she does so the 'statue' himself draws his bow, but the arrow that pierces Sylvia's heart cannot have an immediate effect, and she escapes with her companions into the woods (F, followed by D1).

Dawn breaks. To the music of the *Cortège Rustique*, which was heard in the Prelude, peasants come to the shrine on their way to work and dance before the love-god; piccolos and tambourines are prominent in the music. When they have gone Orion at long last comes from his hiding-place (B), swearing vengeance on the insolent Aminta; finding him apparently dead, he rejoices. A slight noise makes him hide yet again; it is Sylvia, her cold heart turned to love by the god's arrow, searching for her shepherd. She finds him (A1) and, to music heard in the Prelude, tenderly pulls the arrow from his body. But Orion is upon her (B) and carrying her off before she can defend herself.

Peasants find Aminta's body and are sad. But an old sorcerer, entering to an unexpectedly jovial tune, revives Aminta with a rose, and tells him what has happened to Sylvia (B). Aminta appeals to the statue for help, whereupon the 'sorcerer' flings off his great cloak and reveals himself as Eros himself (C); he charges Aminta to save Sylvia.

Act II

After an interlude in which the *Intermezzo* (G) is repeated the curtain goes up on Orion's grotto. Sylvia is inert, thinking only of Aminta (A1 on clarinet). She refuses Orion's attentions (B). For her entertainment he arranges a piquant dance by his Ethiopian slaves.

Sylvia then resorts to guile. She agrees to dance for him, but plies him with drink as she dances.

His attendants all drink too much too. Orion tries to pursue Sylvia as she dances, wishing to embrace her, but falls to the ground in a drunken stupor. Eventually Sylvia is the only person left in the grotto still standing, but unfortunately she cannot find the way out. She appeals to Eros (C), who appears and leads her away; a distant hunting horn (D) suggests that her companions are not far away.

Act III

The scene is the sea-coast, with a temple to Diana at the back. A festival in honour of Bacchus is taking place, and to the famous *Cortège de Bacchus* gods, demi-gods, and peasants join in honouring the wine-god.

When, at the climax, tune L is repeated by the full orchestra Bacchus himself is drawn on in his chariot. Only Aminta is inconsolable (a fragment of A1). Suddenly a ship is sighted; to the music of the barcarolle,

it approaches until Eros can be seen standing in the prow disguised as a pirate; behind him is a familiar veiled figure. The veiled girl lands and dances to the music of the famous Pizzicato; only the tune of the middle section need be given here.

Aminta finds this mysterious dancer irresistible, and in a *pas de deux* he dances with her; Eros raises her veil and reveals her to be Sylvia.

Then follows a *divertissement* in celebration of Sylvia's escape. There is a *Slaves' Dance*, a *Variation-Valse* for Sylvia herself, and a galop for every one. Suddenly Orion appears, raging (B); Sylvia tries to drag Aminta out of harm into the temple (A1), but he insists on standing up to the black hunter. The goddess Diana herself now intervenes and prevents them from fighting; she shoots an arrow into Orion (B), wounding him mortally. When she turns her anger on Aminta for loving above his station Eros shows her a vision of one of her own past indiscretions: her love for the mortal Endymion. Diana, slightly abashed, relents and accepts the gratitude and homage of the lovers, while the orchestra makes one final reference to Sylvia's horn call (D2).

Chapter Five

TCHAIKOVSKY AND THE CLASSICAL BALLET

Swan Lake   The Sleeping Beauty   Nutcracker

In instrumental music, and indeed in some of the other arts, the romantic period follows the classical. It has never been very clear to me why in ballet the order should be reversed. Tchaikovsky does not strike one as being a classical composer. Nevertheless, his ballets are referred to by dancers as classical, presumably because the steps for which they call are the basis of a dancer's technique to-day. They are in any case the best ballets that have yet been written, and so in a very broad sense can be regarded as classics. It is, then, all the more surprising to realize how precarious has been their position in the repertoire. *Swan Lake* had no sort of success in Tchaikovsky's life-time, and he died thinking it was one of his failures, much inferior, he once remarked, to Delibes' *Sylvia*. The great Diaghilev never ventured to present more than half of it (roughly speaking, Acts II and III), and its career in Western Europe as a full-length ballet began at Sadler's Wells Theatre, where it was staged in 1934 with Alicia Markova and Robert Helpmann in the leading parts. Since the War it has been seen in London on numerous occasions, staged not only by our own Sadler's Wells, International, and Festival ballet companies, but also by a number of foreign ones.

Similarly, *The Sleeping Beauty* seemed impracticably long and difficult at the beginning of this century. Diaghilev produced it in London in 1921, but the venture was not wholly successful, and this confirmed Diaghilev in his view that full-length ballets were no longer appreciated, a view that no one would hold to-day. *The Sleeping Beauty* was first given by the Vic-Wells ballet company in 1939, and has been one of their most successful productions ever since. Its revival, like that of *Swan Lake* and *Nutcracker*, was made possible by the presence in this country of Nicholas Sergeyev, who had danced in the Russian productions of the 1890's. *Nutcracker* also had to wait over forty years before London saw it complete in 1934, again at Sadler's Wells. The fact is that these masterpieces have had to overcome the strong feeling, held by ballet-lovers for a matter of centuries, that ballets, unlike operas, are of only passing interest, and that though one might want to see the same dancer over and over again, one certainly did not want to see the same ballet over and over again. When the music is of no interest this attitude is very reasonable, and it is a significant fact that before Diaghilev's day scarcely a single ballet ever survived more than one season on the London stage, however popular. It is, of course, the quality of the music in Tchaikovsky's ballets that makes them bear repetition, in the same way that a good Mozart or Verdi opera bears repetition. Their place in the repertoire is far more secure now than at the beginning of the century.

The structure of the classical ballet differs from anything we have met so far. Roughly speaking, the changes could be rung on the following:

Pas de deux. This is usually a short suite of dances, starting with a fairly long dance for the man and the girl (sometimes called an *adagio*, even when this word is *not* used by the composer to indicate the tempo), followed by two short solo dances, one for each dancer, called *variations* (though not variations in the musical sense), with a vigorous *coda* for both dancers together at the end. The 'Blue Bird' dances in *The Sleeping Beauty* are constructed in this way. A *pas de trois* (for three dancers) might have three solo variations between the opening dance and the coda, as in Act I of *Swan Lake*, and a *pas de six* (for six dancers) six variations in the middle, as in the Prologue to *The Sleeping Beauty*.

Scène. Here the emphasis is on the dramatic situation rather than on pure dancing. Sometimes the characters try to express strong emotion by dancing and miming, but often there are patches in which they just face each other and converse with gestures whose meaning was apparently clear to Russian audiences in the late nineteenth century but is certainly not clear to the average audience in London these days. All these gestures were conventions and were repeated in ballet after ballet.

National Dances. These can hardly be expected to have much connexion with the plot, but they provide opportunities for the *corps de ballet*. Tchaikovsky lived in the great age of the national dance, when almost every country in Europe was asserting its musical individuality. Act III of *Swan Lake* contains a Hungarian czardas, a Polish mazurka, a Spanish bolero, and a Neapolitan dance. *Nutcracker* contains Arabian and Chinese dances. All three ballets contain one full-scale waltz and a number of shorter waltzes, and a sore trial they are to choreographers to-day. The shorter ones can be dealt with without too much trouble, but the longer ones last five or six minutes, and in practice it seems to be very difficult to sustain interest for so long in this rhythm. One feels that at Covent Garden they would like to cut them altogether, but this could hardly be done, for Tchaikovsky had a genius for writing waltzes, and in the suites drawn from the ballets, and long popular in concert-halls, the waltzes are the most popular numbers. For many years Covent Garden took the big waltz in *Swan Lake* from its proper place in the middle of Act I and played it as an *entr'acte* before Act III. In *The Sleeping Beauty* Ashton has devised new choreography for the big waltz, the *corps de ballet* brandishing garlands which seem to suggest romantic rather than classical ballet conventions; the music is usually shortened, and the result is not a success. The Festival Ballet used to end *Nutcracker* with the famous *Valse des Fleurs*, and this was the weakest part of the production. More correctly, and much more successfully, they have now put this waltz back where it belongs, in the middle of the act. Covent Garden has not yet given us this ballet.

Divertissement. In all full-length ballets the plot is padded out with some form of entertainment provided for one of the important characters, and this section, which of course holds up the plot completely, is called the *divertissement*. It provides opportunities for introducing national dances (as in Act III of *Swan Lake*) and 'character' dances (such as those for the cats and Little Red Riding Hood in the last act of *The Sleeping Beauty*). There is also a *divertissement* in the last act of *Coppélia*, and there are two in Britten's *The Prince of the Pagodas*.

Swan Lake (*Le Lac des Cygnes*)

The early history of *Swan Lake* is somewhat complex. In the summer of 1871 Tchaikovsky spent a holiday with his sister and amused himself concocting a little ballet for her children. The music has never been published, and it would be interesting to know if it still survives in Russia. In 1875 the Bolshoi Theatre in Moscow commissioned Tchaikovsky to write a ballet, and he persuaded them to accept as plot the theme he had chosen for his sister's children, the theme we now know as *Swan Lake,* said to be based on an old Germanic legend. He finished the first two acts in a fortnight, but his enthusiasm must have waned when he discovered the reaction to his music of those responsible for the production. The conductor said he had never in his life seen such complicated ballet music, while the choreographer thought it so unsuitable for dancing that he cut out about a third of the music and replaced it with hack pieces of no musical interest. There had never been a ballet in Russia with good music; good music was not what people in the dancing world wanted. It is not surprising that when the ballet was first performed in March 1877 the indifference felt towards it by those behind the curtain affected the front of the house as well; after a few bad performances the ballet was dropped, to the relief of every one.

During the next few years Tchaikovsky's reputation as a composer rose rapidly, and in 1882 some one in Moscow apparently felt that his position was established sufficiently to justify a revival of *Swan Lake.* Little seems to be known of this production, except that it was no more successful than the first one.

In 1893 Tchaikovsky died, world-famous, and a little later the great choreographer Marius Petipa, who had just had a notable success with *The Sleeping Beauty,* revived Act II of *Swan Lake* (February 1894), and then (January 1895) the whole ballet, with many alterations of his own, at the Maryinsky Theatre, St Petersburg. By this time Petipa was an old man, and though he roughed out a general plan for the choreography, more particularly for the first and third acts, he left the details to his assistant, Lev Ivanov. This is the version that British and American companies have always staged, and most people regard it as sacred. But of this more in a moment.

We are now in a better position to discuss scores and recordings.

Scores. 1. A full score published by Jurgenson. This is extremely rare; but though palpably earlier than Petipa's version, it does not represent that of 1877 either. There is an appendix consisting of a single piece, a *Danse Russe.* The only reason for relegating music to an appendix is that it was omitted in what seems to the publisher the most important recent production. But, as we have seen, a third of the ballet would have qualified for the appendix after the original 1877 production. In any case, I doubt if Tchaikovsky's reputation was then sufficient to encourage the publication of such a very large score. It thus seems safe to guess that this score represents the 1882 revival, in which all the music except the *Danse Russe* was presumably given.

2. A piano arrangement of Petipa's version published in 1895 by Jurgenson. This has been reproduced, apparently photographically, by Novello and, more recently and at more than twice the price, by the Tchaikovsky Foundation of New York. (All three editions contain the same misprints.) I must add that the American version contains piano arrangements of nearly all the music which Petipa cut. Petipa's cuts, additions, and rearrangement of the order of the dances will be discussed later.

3. In 1951 Broude Brothers of New York issued a reproduction of the Jurgenson full score, with the addition of the three Drigo pieces (though not the polka).

Recordings. The ballet as presumably danced in 1882—that is, as found in the rare Jurgenson full score—can be heard complete on Mercury MRL 2528-30, a most enterprising set of discs. But those brought up on the Covent Garden production must be prepared to forgo such Petipa-devised dances as the so-called 'Black Swan' sequence. The ballet as usually danced to-day—that is, in the Petipa version—can be heard, slightly cut, on Decca LXT 2681-82.

It should now be clear that Petipa's choreography, though rightly admired and loved, was not conceived with the music, as was his choreography for *The Sleeping Beauty*. There is thus no reason to regard it as sacrosanct, and indeed there is every justification for the

Odette and Siegfried

Bolshoi Ballet's re-creation of the choreography. The truth is that the original choreography has long been forgotten and was probably not worth remembering. Petipa paid
no more heed to it than he did to the original score. Here are his more important
alterations:

> Act I. *Pas de deux* cut and used in Act III. Waltz and *pas de trois* change places; the waltz
> originally came second, after the opening Introduction.
>
> Act II. The famous *pas de deux* in G flat (labelled *Scène* in the score) originally came near the
> end of the act; Petipa put it in the middle.
>
> Act III. Petipa cut a dance for the *corps de ballet* and some nurses after the opening *Scène*,
> also a long *pas de six* standing just before the national dances, and a *Danse Russe*. He
> built up the 'Black Swan' dances from the *pas de deux* in Act I, and instructed Drigo,
> his conductor, to orchestrate a Tchaikovsky piano piece as a variation for the ballerina.
>
> Act IV. Petipa got Drigo to orchestrate two more of Tchaikovsky's piano pieces, which were
> inserted after the opening scene and after the andante introduction to the Finale.

It is substantially Petipa's version that is danced at Covent Garden, and, for that matter,
by all ballet companies in Western Europe and America. His instinct rightly led him to
shorten Act I, which is badly lacking in plot, and build up the character of Odile, in whom
Tchaikovsky seems to have taken no interest. But his additions to the last act seem to me
indefensible; their mood cuts right across the situation, which is so admirably reflected
in the rest of the music.

In the following synopsis the Petipa version (as emended at Covent Garden) is described.
A vertical line in the margin indicates what can be found on the Decca recording.

There is only one leitmotiv: the swan theme, first heard at the end of Act I.

Act I

One might have expected Tchaikovsky to begin with the famous swan theme. In fact, he starts his Introduction with a surprisingly similar theme, in the same mood of sad longing and twilight melancholy, and played, as is the other, by the oboe.

Scène. We see a park with a castle at the back. Prince Siegfried and his friends are drinking at tables on the grass. It is his birthday, and peasants congratulate him (quiet oboes over drone bass, presumably an imitation of peasant bagpipes).

Pas de Trois. He is entertained with dances. The first of the four variations in the middle, the one in G minor, is usually cut; of the three remaining variations the vigorous one in the middle is for the man.

Scène. Brass instruments announce the arrival of the Princess, Siegfried's mother. In mime she tells him it is time he chose a wife; he is sad, thinking marriage would be the end of his carefree life.

Waltz. The famous waltz that comes in the orchestral concert suite. Covent Garden now dance it as a *pas de six* to new choreography.

Pas d'Action. Siegfried's tutor, Wolfgang, who has been drinking too much, gives a ridiculous imitation of the previous dances and falls over.

Scène (very short) and Danse des Coupes. As daylight fails every one joins in a grand, vigorous polonaise, while the prince sits wrapped in gloom. Note the glockenspiel in the middle section.

Scène. A flight of swans is seen (A); the prince, his imagination fired, determines to pursue them.

Act II: The Lakeside

Scène. A is repeated in fuller form, as a prelude.

Scène. Benno and other friends of Siegfried come into the dark glade in search of the wild swans. Siegfried follows and suddenly sees the swans, though only momentarily (A, bar 2). Later, alone on the stage, he is confronted by the Swan Queen herself. "Why do you persecute me?" she mimes.

All through the ballet the oboe is associated with her.

As the music grows in excitement she explains that her name is Odette, and that she has been condemned by a wicked magician called Rothbart to be a swan, except that she can resume human form between midnight and dawn. Only a man's love can release her from the spell.

Suddenly Rothbart, disguised as an owl, is seen menacing them (fortissimo climax on brass) Odette stops Siegfried from trying to shoot the owl. He pledges his troth, and they leave the glade.

Scène. A *corps de ballet* of swans glide in, happy for their brief hours in human form.

The huntsmen, returning, mistake them for swans as they cluster together, frightened, at the side of the stage, and Siegfried arrives only just in time to save them from being shot. Odette herself reappears (quiet music, a high flute solo) and calms their fluttering spirits.

Dance of the Swans. A waltz by the *corps de ballet.*

This suave tune is followed by more animated phrases on flute, oboe, clarinet, and bassoon in turn.

Scène. The famous G flat *pas de deux* for Siegfried and Odette, with the swan girls joining in the more animated sections.

(Tchaikovsky took this theme from an unsuccessful opera about a water nymph, called *Undine.*) The title of this long piece suggests that in the original version of the ballet it was mimed rather than danced. It starts with a harp solo.

Dance of the Swans. This is the title in the piano arrangements, but the piece is usually called *The Dance of the Little Swans.* It is very short and is danced by four of the younger members of the *corps de ballet,* their arms linked.

Danse Générale. G, more grandly orchestrated, and danced by all the swan girls, two of whom are especially prominent.

Scène. A short dance for Odette.

Coda. This is the coda to all the swan dances, which originally constituted a separate group in which Siegfried made no appearance. He returns at the end, with Benno and the other huntsmen, and the act closes with a repeat of the swan music (A) and, at its climax (but only in some productions), a reappearance of the menacing but never very convincing owl.

Odile dances with Siegfried, while Rothbart looks on

ACT III: THE GREAT HALL OF SIEGFRIED'S CASTLE
(The Decca LP recording has the Act I waltz here as an *entr'acte*, as in the late 1940's at Covent Garden.)

Scène. Siegfried's mother is giving a ball; the guests arrive to stately music.

Scène. Trumpets announce more guests, and soon six prospective brides are dancing a ceremonial waltz, hoping for Siegfried's favour. The waltz is memorable for one gloriously crunchy chord.

Siegfried is listless and uninterested, though he joins in.

Scène. The Princess takes her son aside and asks him which of the girls pleases him most.

It can hardly be a coincidence that this tune resembles K; it is dramatically right that it should. There are more trumpet calls for the arrival of the nefarious Baron Rothbart with his daughter Odile, whom he has disguised as Odette. She is dressed in black. (In modern productions she is danced by the same ballerina as Odette.) Siegfried is struck by the likeness (A).

In the original version it is at this point that the *pas de six* occurs, presumably danced by the six prospective brides. Then follows a *divertissement* of national dances, for which the excuse is the entertainment of Siegfried and his guests.

Divertissement

> *Bolero*. Tchaikovsky hoped, vainly, that the dancers would play the castanets themselves.
>
> *Neapolitan Dance*. This begins with a cornet solo; the second half is a tarantella. Often cut.
>
> *Hungarian Dance: Czardas*. This starts in melancholy vein and ends very vigorously; here Tchaikovsky was undoubtedly inspired by the czardas in *Coppélia*. This comes in the orchestral suite.
>
> *Mazurka*. A vigorous Polish dance.

Pas de Deux. The so-called 'Black Swan' dances: Siegfried, captivated by Odile, dances a waltz with her.

Then comes a variation for Odile (violin solo) and another (usually cut) for Siegfried; all this music was taken by Petipa from Act I. Now follow two of Petipa's interpolations: a polka[1] (N1) for Siegfried and an orchestration of Tchaikovsky's piano piece, *L'Espiègle* (Op. 72, No. 12), for Odile (N2).

Finally there is the coda, which originally appeared in Act I. It is here that the dancer has to execute thirty-two *fouettés*; this seemed very much more difficult in 1900 than it does now.

Scène. The Princess is delighted at Siegfried's choice (L). Then comes a brief reference to the waltz of the brides (K), which only has relevance if Siegfried has *not* just danced the *pas de deux* with Odile; in the original ballet this was the only time he did dance with her. To general approval Rothbart joins the hand of his black-hearted daughter to that of the Prince, and as the music rises in excitement the real Odette (though, unhappily, the less real for having to be mimed by some other dancer) is seen at a window vainly trying to warn Siegfried of his danger. As the marriage arrangements are completed the orchestra thunders out the swan theme (A), and the hall is plunged into sudden darkness; Siegfried, aware too late that he has been deceived, hurries out in the desperate hope of saving Odette.

---

[1] This little piece is described in the piano score published by the Tchaikovsky Foundation of New York as probably by Drigo himself, and it is claimed that this is its first publication. In fact it is by Tchaikovsky, and comes in the original Jurgenson full score as an extra section tacked on to Odile's variation (the violin solo); this polka also starts and ends as a violin solo, with lots of double-stopping. Petipa (or Drigo) just picked out the middle section, which consists of the tune used in the polka played by the full orchestra; the full version has probably never been played in this country, and it has never been published in any of the piano arrangements.

ACT IV: BY THE LAKESIDE

Entr'acte. Tchaikovsky lifted this from his unsuccessful opera, *The Voyevoda*, but it is sometimes cut, and the *Dance of the Little Swans*, from later in this act, used as an *entr'acte* instead.

Next, Petipa interpolated Drigo's orchestration of Tchaikovsky's piano piece, *Valse Bluette* (Op. 72, No. 11).

Scène. The swan girls cannot understand what has happened to Odette.

Dance of the Little Swans. This is not to be confused with the better known dance of the same name in Act II. It is a lovely piece, with rather more Russian feeling than is to be found elsewhere in the ballet.

Scène. To agitated music Odette runs in and tells the swan girls that they are betrayed, and that all is lost; the scene grows dark, and a thunderstorm begins.

Scène Finale. During the noble Introduction Siegfried arrives. Then comes the last of the Petipa-Drigo interpolations; this is an orchestration of another piano piece by Tchaikovsky —a mazurka called *Un poco di Chopin* (Op. 72, No. 15)—to which Siegfried and Odette dance a sad farewell.

The swan theme (A) returns in agitated form. As Siegfried asks Odette for forgiveness Rothbart appears; Siegfried drives him away. But Odette, in despair, has thrown herself into the lake; Siegfried also drowns himself. In the words of the Covent Garden programme note, "This supreme sacrifice breaks the spell, and, as the curtain falls, the Prince and Odette are seen sailing away reunited in another kingdom."

The end of this ballet is as confused as the very similar end of *Giselle.* In the 1877 version the Prince and Odette were reunited at the bottom of the lake. Act II also has a superficial resemblance to *Giselle*, and at first sight *Swan Lake* would seem to be just another in a long, long line of ballets about ethereal creatures dancing in the pale moonlight amid the dark trees by the water's edge. The difference is that for the first time this conventional situation is distilled in the music. Could any other composer have captured the slightly breathless, moonlit, Corot-like quality of the three pieces, each called *Scène*, at the start of Act II? Or the tragic urgency of the final music? This may be a classical ballet in the technical sense, but musically it is the most romantically lovely of all ballets.

Despite the brilliance of the national dances, Act III is not wholly successful. The composer makes little attempt to portray either the bad baron or his evil daughter, and they should have been very important characters; Petipa could not entirely remedy the fault.

We need not regret the cutting of the *pas de six* in this act, for it is poor music, but the *Danse Russe* might be worth reviving.[1]

It would be silly to be too disparaging about the Drigo interpolations, for they are well orchestrated and eminently danceable. But a performance of the original version of the music, with new choreography, would be welcome.

The Sleeping Beauty

Score. Of the original Jurgenson full score there seems never to have been more than one copy in circulation in this country. A full score in four volumes was published in Moscow in 1952. Jurgenson published a piano arrangement just before the first performance in 1890, and this is reproduced photographically in the version published by the Tchaikovsky Foundation of New York, the only one now obtainable.
Recordings. The entire ballet as given in the recent Moscow full score is given on Mercury MRL 2524-27. Almost the entire ballet as given at Covent Garden (where a number of cuts are made) is available on the much more economical H.M.V. CLP 1073-74, very well played by the Covent Garden Orchestra under Robert Irving.

The book was based on the story by Charles Perrault called *La Belle au Bois dormant.* When Diaghilev presented the ballet in London in 1921 he called it *The Sleeping Princess,* having been advised that people would think it was a pantomime if he called it *The Sleeping Beauty.* Years later Covent Garden retained Diaghilev's title for a few seasons, but have since reverted to the proper title. The first performance was given in January 1890 at the Maryinsky Theatre, St Petersburg, with choreography by Marius Petipa, who had adapted the story and who directed the composer as to the style and length of each dance. The orchestra was conducted by Drigo.

There are two important leitmotivs: an angry one for the wicked fairy, Carabosse,

and a gracious one for the good Lilac Fairy.

The chord progression at the start of Carabosse's tune becomes very important later.

PROLOGUE: IN THE PALACE OF KING FLORESTAN XXIV
Introduction. A followed by B; at the end the curtain rises.
March. The baby Princess Aurora is to be christened; guests arrive for the ceremony and are shown to their places by Cattalabutte, the Master of Ceremonies.

This tune sounds very effective later, played quietly low on the cornet.
Scène Dansante. The six fairy godmothers arrive to the strains of a waltz.

---

[1] Tchaikovsky thought so; he used the tune for a piece of the same name in the *Twelve Pieces for Pianoforte,* Op. 40, and he used the first half of the *Neapolitan Dance* in his *Twenty-four easy Pianoforte Pieces,* Op. 39. Probably this too had been cut in 1877. Both these sets of piano pieces appeared in 1878.

So far there has been no dancing—only miming. But when the pages and young girls have presented their gifts they dance briefly to another waltz.

Pas de Six. The fairy godmothers are the last to give their presents.

After this extended piece each godmother dances a short solo variation. I give first their names as they appear in the score, and then, in brackets, those used at Covent Garden. (Diaghilev invented yet another set.)

Candite (*The Fairy of the Crystal Fountain*).

Coulante; Fleur de Farine (*The Fairy of the Enchanted Garden*).
Miettes qui tombent (*The Fairy of the Woodland Glade*).

Canari qui chantent (*The Fairy of the Songbirds*). This is the famous finger variation, largely a piccolo solo.
Violente (*The Fairy of the Golden Vine*).
La Fée des Lilas (*The Lilac Fairy*).

A coda for all the fairies completes the *pas de six.*

Finale. Just before the Lilac Fairy can present her gift there are ominous sounds outside, and the Fairy Carabosse arrives in a chariot pulled by rats (B). She is old and very horrid, and furious that she has not been invited to be one of the godmothers. The King rather meanly puts all the blame on the wretched Cattalabutte, and she beats him savagely. Much worse, she foretells that one day the Princess shall die by pricking her finger on a spindle (A, very prominent). Eventually the Lilac Fairy comes forward and undertakes to change the Princess's death to a deep sleep a hundred years long, to be ended by a Prince's kiss; this hope of eventual salvation is her gift to the baby. Her calm, graceful music (B) is briefly interrupted by the growling, irritable sounds (deriving from A) of Carabosse getting back into her chariot and driving off in a huff.

ACT I: SIXTEEN YEARS LATER; THE GROUNDS AND COLONNADES OF THE PALACE

Scène. It is Aurora's birthday, and the palace grounds fill with people who have come from the neighbouring countryside to celebrate the event. Among them are some women whom Cattalabutte catches threading spindles; horrified, he sends them packing, and, at the end, the orchestra makes his reason clear (A1).

Waltz. This is the famous waltz that comes in the concert suite. A glockenspiel is prominent in one of the episodes. At Covent Garden it is danced by village girls.

Scène (very short). Aurora's entrance. Four princes have come to compete for her hand in marriage.

Pas d'Action. The famous *Rose Adagio* of the concert suite. After a harp solo we hear

The four princes in turn present Aurora with a rose. Three shorter dances follow: one for the maids of honour, later joined by the pages.

There follows a variation for Aurora; then, after a cadenza for solo violin, comes this tune:

Finally a coda, in which the tension seems to mount.

As this tune works up to a climax Aurora meets an old woman in the crowd, a suspicious-looking creature who shows her a spindle, which is something she has never seen before. At the point where the rhythm changes to that of a waltz Aurora takes the spindle and dances gaily round, holding it; at the climax she pricks her finger on it (A1 loud and slow on the trombones). There has been no break in the music, but at this moment, when the mood darkens, the Finale has begun. In a short, hectic little dance, the tempo getting quicker and quicker, Aurora spins round in her agony and falls to the ground, apparently lifeless. We hear A1 on the trombones in a new form.

The old hag flings back her hood, and Carabosse's theme in its original form (A) leaves no doubt of her identity. The princes try to seize her; but there is a crash, she disappears, and they run off frightened. The Lilac Fairy appears (B) and waves her wand over the decaying palace. The music rises to a tremendous climax; the great chords of her spell promising salvation clearly derive from the evil chords associated with Carabosse.

As her theme returns, the violins suggest the weeds and undergrowth that can already be seen rising to shroud the lifeless palace. (Much of this passage is cut at Covent Garden; from the musical point of view this is a pity.)

Act II: A Hundred Years Later; a Forest Glade

Entr'acte and Scène. Horn calls provide the conventional indication that a hunt is in progress. Among the huntsmen is Prince Desiré (more happily named Florimund at Covent Garden), and there are also ladies present. Soon some diversions are proposed:

Colin-Maillard (Blind-man's Buff). Scurrying music.
Scène. This is very short.
Dance of the Duchesses. An old-fashioned minuet.
Dance of the Baronesses. Cut at Covent Garden.
Dance of the Countesses.
Dance of the Marquises.
Farandole. This is preceded by a brief introduction. One wonders whether the title is a mistake; the music is marked *tempo di mazurka* and is much more like a mazurka than a farandole.

Scène. The horn calls that started the act are heard again as the hunting party moves off. The Prince, who has been blind to the blandishments of the court ladies, remains in melancholy mood. As the light fails the Lilac Fairy glides in on a boat of mother-of-pearl (B on the flute, with one note altered. Every listener must feel that this alteration is for the worse, and it is strange that Tchaikovsky should have made it). She conjures up for the Prince a vision of Aurora, and tells him her story.

Pas d'Action. The vision dances with the Prince in the glade to a tune that surely derives from the slow movement of Tchaikovsky's Fifth Symphony.

Towards the end the music quickens, and we hear this same tune in a new rhythm.

Then follows a variation for Aurora.

This lovely tune exists in two orchestrations: at Covent Garden as a solo for the violins; in the new Moscow full score as an oboe solo. In the coda that follows the vision of Aurora vanishes.

Scène. The Prince calls on the Lilac Fairy to help him find the Sleeping Beauty. (This short piece is cut at Covent Garden.)

Panorama. The Prince follows the Lilac Fairy deep into the wood. (This comes in the concert suite; the tune is in three-four, the accompaniment in six-eight.)

At this point Act II ends, as given at Covent Garden; but this was not the wish of Petipa or Tchaikovsky, who planned that the Awakening should be the climax of Act II and not the opening of Act III. To cover the change of scene, Tchaikovsky wrote an attractive *entr'acte* in which a solo violin has the most interesting part; this is cut at Covent Garden, where it is maintained that the music is too quiet to hide the noise of the scenery being changed, and there is, of course, no occasion to play it if the Awakening is postponed until after the last interval. Let us accept the rearrangement with no more than a raised eyebrow.

ACT III
Scene 1: Transformation Scene; the Awakening.

The scene opens with what is justly called a 'symphonic *entr'acte*,' in which the composer binds together the spell theme (N3), Carabosse's theme (A), and the Lilac Fairy's (B), all played quietly beneath shimmering high C's endlessly repeated by the violins. When the curtain rises we at first see rolling clouds (or at least, we should), and these dissolve to reveal the palace overgrown with weeds. Soon the Lilac Fairy comes into view, slowly leading the mystified Prince. The music rises to a climax, and at a great blow on the gong the Prince kisses the sleeping figure. At once the weeds begin to vanish as life returns to the palace. (Much of the finale to this scene is cut at Covent Garden.)

Scene 2: The Palace; the Wedding.

March. At Covent Garden most of this is played as an *entr'acte*, to allow the stage to be tidied up after the Awakening.

Polacca. During this stately dance all the fairy-tale characters that are shortly to entertain the Prince and his bride parade round the stage. (A polacca is a polonaise.)

Pas de Quatre. Two of the four solo variations, those for the Gold and Sapphire Fairies, have surprisingly poor music and are sensibly cut at Covent Garden, where what is left is described as 'Florestan and his two Sisters.' (This Florestan is apparently no relation to Aurora's father.) First comes an *Intrada*.

The variation for the Silver Fairy is a polka (note the glockenspiel).

This is followed by a variation for the Diamond Fairy (note the triangle), and then a coda for all three dancers.

Puss-in-Boots and the White Cat. This comes in the concert suite. Oboe and bassoons imitate the miaows, and pizzicato strings the spitting.

Pas de Quatre. These dances were originally for Cinderella, Prince Fortuné, the Blue Bird, and Princess Florine, but at a very early stage they became a *pas de deux* for the Blue Birds:

Opening piece for both dancers. Flute, and later flute answered by clarinet, swoop like blue tits.

Variation for the male Blue Bird. A vigorous waltz; note the syncopation.

Variation for the female Blue Bird. Flutes imitate bird song.

Coda for both dancers.

Pas de Caractère: Little Red Riding Hood and the Wolf. The woodwind show us Red Riding Hood hurrying through the wood; soon wolf-growls are heard low on the strings, and in fear she increases her pace. (At Covent Garden the wolf always comes in much sooner than the composer intended.)

Then comes a considerable quantity of music that seems always to be cut: *Hop-o'-my-Thumb and the Ogre*, and *Cinderella and Prince Fortuné* (the two full scores do not agree as to their order). Covent Garden also cuts the Introduction and the short first movement of the ensuing *pas de deux*, and thus goes straight from *Little Red Riding Hood* to the adagio.

Pas de Deux. Here is the music of the adagio.

This is followed by the Prince's variation, Aurora's variation (yet another violin solo),

and the coda.

This gay and very Russian tune is repeated over and over again with ingenious new harmonies and orchestration. It must have been intended for the Prince and Aurora, but Diaghilev christened it 'The Three Ivans' and had it danced by three men in peasant costumes, squatting on their haunches and shooting their legs out *à la russe*. Covent Garden follow this tradition, which is certainly very effective.

The following dance (a rather dull, old-fashioned saraband) is always cut.

Finale and Apotheosis. All the characters in this act parade in turn to the strains of a vigorous mazurka.

For the final Apotheosis, in which the Lilac Fairy reappears, Tchaikovsky used a French tune popular early in the nineteenth century (but much older than that), called *Vive Henri Quatre*. I quote it with the original words, though they are not, of course, sung in the ballet.

The Sleeping Beauty is Tchaikovsky's longest and most integrated ballet. Though there is, perhaps, nothing which touches the heart as much as certain moments in Act II of *Swan Lake*, the music is more consistently good. The orchestration is luxuriant and, one would think, fascinating to play; in short, the whole ballet can reasonably be regarded as Tchaikovsky's masterpiece.

Much of the credit must go to Petipa. He knew what he could get out of dancers, and he also knew what he could get out of Tchaikovsky. For the 'cat' dance he asked for "Repeated mewing. Caresses and blows. At the end, claws scratching and squawling. Start off three-four *amoroso*. End up in three-four with mewing, becoming quicker and quicker." For the Diamond Fairy he asked for "Showers of diamonds, like electric sparks, two-four *vivo*." In each case Tchaikovsky gave Petipa exactly what he asked for, and there can be no doubt that Petipa was capable of finding words which would touch off the composer's imagination. Not that Tchaikovsky always obeyed servilely. Sometimes he flouted the choreographer's wishes, or—more probably—talked him out of them. Sometimes he obeyed the letter rather than the spirit, as when Petipa demanded a chromatic scale from the whole orchestra at the point where the old hag who gives Aurora the spindle flings off her hood and reveals herself as Carabosse. The chromatic scale is there, but it is far from noticeable, and Tchaikovsky has much better ways of conveying the situation. The directions for the 'Blue Bird' dances are particularly interesting. Tchaikovsky did, however, follow Petipa scrupulously when an accompaniment to mime was required. For instance, at the start of Act I Cattalabutte catches the women threading spindles and brings them up before the King. Here are Petipa's instructions:

Question: "Where are you taking them?" (Four bars.)
Answer: "To prison." (Four bars.)
Question: "What have they done?" (Four bars.)
Answer: He points to the knitting-needles. (Four bars.)

This is how Tchaikovsky set about the first question and answer (pp. 55-56 in the piano score); the other question and answer have similar music.

It would be difficult to convey better in music the upward inflection of the voice, when asking a question, and Cattalabutte's garrulous replies. But then the whole score is full of superb examples of descriptive music. Tchaikovsky would have made an unparalleled writer of film music; he would have taken in his stride the sort of instructions that modern composers so frequently accept —"47 seconds of music for suspense in an empty house," "53 seconds for climbing up on to the battlements," or whatever it is. Petipa's requirements were very similar to those of a modern film director.

In 1921 Stravinsky wrote an open letter to Diaghilev on the eve of the first performance of *The Sleeping Princess* at the Alhambra, London. In it he wrote of Tchaikovsky:

> This cultured man, with his knowledge of folk song and of old French music, had no need to engage in archæological research in order to present the age of Louis XIV; he recreated the character of the period by his musical language, preferring involuntary but living anachronisms to conscious and laboured pasticcio; a virtue that appertains only to great creative minds. I have just read again the score of this ballet. I have instrumented some numbers of it which had remained unorchestrated and unperformed. I have spent some days of intense pleasure in finding therein again and again the same feeling of freshness, inventiveness, ingenuity, and vigour.

I had always wondered why Tchaikovsky should have ended the ballet with a splendid but rather uncharacteristic tune in a minor key, and it was only by chance that I came on *Vive Henri Quatre* in an old book of French songs. Between about 1750 and 1850 the tune was published on many occasions. Dussek wrote variations on it, and Sir Henry Bishop composed an opera about Henri IV in which the tune occurs frequently. Quite apart from the fact that it is a wonderful tune, its associations make it just right for its position in *The Sleeping Beauty*. Are there any other old French tunes in the ballet, one wonders? There is an example in the opera *Pique-Dame* (taken from Grétry's opera *Richard Cœur de Lion*), and a pseudo-old French song in *Eugen Onegin* (*Triquet's Couplets*), and we shall find Tchaikovsky showing some interest in French folk-songs in his last ballet. But I doubt if any more will be discovered in *The Sleeping Beauty*, unless it turns out that the *Dance of the Duchesses* or the saraband were suggested by some eighteenth-century phrase.

Stravinsky's remarks on his own orchestrations are tantalizingly incomplete. I can only mention that, in the recent Moscow score, the orchestration of Aurora's variation in Act II and of the Apotheosis music is quite different from the versions played at Covent Garden, which suggests that there may have been no definitive version of these two sections. Were they perhaps composed in piano score and included in the published piano arrangement, but later cut by Petipa, and so never orchestrated by Tchaikovsky? In the Moscow full score the tune of the Apotheosis is heard twice (as in the piano arrangement); at its first appearance a piano is prominent (though, regrettably, not used in the Mercury complete recording).

It is tempting to think that those numbers with a piano in them might have been scored by Stravinsky, who has always been addicted to using pianos in the orchestra, but it is hard to believe that the Silver Fairy variation (which has a piano) was not danced in the original version. It is more likely that Petipa cut the Act II variation because there had already been enough of the vision, and turned down the minor-key ending to the ballet as being too unconventional. It should be remembered that the piano arrangement appeared before the first performance of the ballet and thus did not include any late alterations.

Nutcracker (Casse Noisette)

Scores. The old Jurgenson full score, long unprocurable, and the new Moscow one are similar; again, the piano score recently issued by the Tchaikovsky Foundation of New York turns out to be a reproduction of the original and now very rare Jurgenson one.
Recording. Every note of the ballet is splendidly recorded on Mercury MRL 2508-9.

Nutcracker is based on a story by E. T. A. Hoffmann (who was also responsible for the plot of *Coppélia*) called *Nutcracker and Mouse King,* but Tchaikovsky seems to have used a French version by Dumas. Tchaikovsky felt little interest in the story, which is hardly surprising, and composed with difficulty. The first performance took place within a year of the composer's death, in December 1892, again at the Maryinsky Theatre, St Petersburg, and, as later with *Swan Lake,* the choreography was roughed out by Petipa, but executed by his assistant Lev Ivanov. It was given complete at Sadler's Wells (before either of the other Tchaikovsky ballets) as early as 1934, but it has never been staged at Covent Garden; indeed, it has never been such a success as the others. For some years the Festival Ballet made it moderately attractive in a production that departed widely from the intentions of both Ivanov and Tchaikovsky, and then for the first time, at Christmas 1957, demonstrated that Ivanov and Tchaikovsky knew best by restaging it, with surprising success, in a version much closer to the original. It seems clear now that the ballet can only succeed if the emphasis is on the children; and the children must be real children, not fully-trained ballet-dancers doing their best to look ten years younger than they are.

This is the only ballet mentioned in this book which has no leitmotivs.

ACT I
Scene 1: A Room in the 'President's' House
Overture. Tchaikovsky achieves lightness by dispensing with the cellos and double-basses.
Scène. (As in *Swan Lake,* the composer uses the title *Scène* for music which is mimed rather than danced.) The 'President' and his wife are decorating a Christmas tree with their guests. (In the Festival Ballet production we at first see only the children, trying to peep through the door to find out what the grown-ups are doing.) When the tree is ready the children come rushing in (clarinets and bassoons in quick six-eight time over a drum roll). They are struck with wonder by the great tree (oboe and harp).
March. At the President's suggestion the children march round pretending to be soldiers. This is the famous march that comes in the concert suite.

Galop, etc. Tired of marching, the children dance a galop. (The Festival Ballet make this a solo for Clara, the small daughter of the house.)

This is interrupted by the return of their parents in fancy dress, to an old-fashioned tune.

The Battle of the Toy Soldiers and the Mice

Soon the grown-ups are dancing to a well-known French traditional song (here transposed down from F to D for those prepared to sing it).

On the last appearance of this tune the trumpet plays the second half.

Scène Dansante. Enter Councillor Drosselmeyer, a cranky old gentleman with a passion for mechanical toys; he is characterized by a dry, fantastic tune in which a falling seventh is prominent.

The children, at first frightened, are reassured when he fetches in some presents (E again): two boxes, one shaped like a cabbage and the other like a pie. When his falling seventh finds itself in waltz rhythm

a doll and a soldier emerge from the boxes and dance a waltz.

By way of coda there is a fascinating presto in rumba rhythm.

Scène, etc. Drosselmeyer has given to his host's daughter, Clara (Marie in Hoffmann's original), a nutcracker, which her brother, Fritz, covets. At first she is delighted with it.

But at the climax of this tune Fritz breaks it. (Tchaikovsky rightly avoids a tragic note here.) Clara sings a lullaby to her toy.

The same bar of accompaniment is repeated all through this melody; its accordion flavour reminds one of a dance in the last scene of *Petrushka*. Clara's lullaby is twice interrupted by Fritz and the boys aggressively playing soldiers and annoying the girls (trumpet and drum). To put an end to the squabbling, the President suggests that the grown-ups shall dance the traditional *Gross-Vater*.

(This tune is used by Schumann at the end of both *Papillons* and *Carnaval*, where it is described as *Thème du XVIIième siècle*.) The final tag, based on the notes marked with a square bracket, also comes in *Papillons* and is traditionally repeated over and over again, faster and faster; this is what happens to it in *Nutcracker*.

Scène (Side 2). To the strains of Clara's lullaby (K) the guests depart (though in the Festival Ballet production Drosselmeyer stays till the end of the scene). The sleepy children go to bed; the lullaby tune is last played by the cor anglais. Soon Clara returns to the empty, moonlit room in her night clothes. She cannot sleep and wants to see her broken nutcracker once more. The dark frightens her. The clock strikes twelve, and she hears mice in the wainscot (bass clarinet and bassoons low, with squeaks on the piccolo). Suddenly the Christmas tree begins to grow larger and larger (to a phrase on the violins ascending in sequence), and as the music gets louder Clara becomes more and more frightened.

Scène. By now we are presumably sharing her nightmare. A miniature battle is heralded by a sentinel calling, "Who goes there?" There is a sudden bang, and toy soldiers (brass) and the mice (piccolo squeaks) join battle, Nutcracker leading the soldiers and the Mouse King the mice. It is rather a long battle, and just before the only soft passage, which comes right at the end, Clara saves the day by throwing her slipper at the Mouse King; immediately the mice scurry away, leaving Nutcracker and his men in possession of the field. Nutcracker changes into a handsome prince and invites Clara to accompany him to the Kingdom of Sweets.

Scene 2: A Forest
The Prince and Clara make their way through the forest to this tune.

Waltz of the Snowflakes. This is rather long; it is enlivened after some time by a chorus of girls or children, singing this wordless tune:

(The Festival Ballet omit the vocal line.)

Act II: At the Court of the Sugar-plum Fairy

The Chinese Dance from the Divertissement

Scène. When this tune is repeated high on the violins, playing harmonics (with the harp and celeste), the curtain rises, and the Sugar-plum Fairy appears. The music dies away and leads without a break into a new *scène*.

Scène. Clara and the Prince arrive in a boat to the sound of what is called 'flutter-tonguing' on the flutes. Soon Clara is telling the Sugar-plum Fairy their story in mime, and we hear again, briefly, the battle rhythm low on the bass strings and the mouse squeaks on the piccolo. To the sound of woodwind and brass (no strings) a sumptuous feast is spread for the visitors, and the dances that follow are for their entertainment.

Divertissement

    Chocolate. From Spain; an enchantingly vulgar trumpet solo.

    Coffee. From Arabia; low, mysterious Oriental sounds.
    Tea. From China; high flutes over low, trotting bassoons.
    Bouffon. A Russian trepak; very vigorous.
    Les Mirlitons (*The Reed-pipes*). The first section is for three flutes with, later, a cor anglais solo; the middle section starts with the brass and percussion alone.

Mother Gigogne. Over a tambourine accompaniment this music is heard:

This is probably a French folk-song; for the middle section the composer uses *Cadet Rousselle*:

Then Q returns, but quicker.

Waltz of the Flowers. First an introduction with prominent harp part; then a full-length waltz with the horns and clarinets sharing the main tune.
Pas de Deux. For the Prince and The Sugar-plum Fairy.

The main section, magnificent music:

Variation for the Prince: a tarantella.
Variation for the Sugar-plum Fairy: the famous celeste solo. The final section of this dance never seems to be played.
Coda for both dancers.

Final Waltz and Apotheosis. One of Tchaikovsky's most virile waltz tunes.

Unfortunately the episodes do not quite reach this level. The Apotheosis is based on O; Cyril Beaumont says it represents a bee-hive guarded by flying bees, but it does not in the Festival Ballet production.

E

Tchaikovsky was in Paris shortly before the first performance of *Nutcracker*, and there he was shown one of the first celestes ever to be made. He was so delighted with the tone of this tinkling miniature piano that he had one smuggled secretly into Russia. During rehearsals every one was sworn to secrecy, so that the Sugar-plum Fairy's variation could make its maximum effect; the new sound quality did in fact take the audience by surprise, and it made a big impression. It has also ensured the popularity of the famous concert suite, which consists of the Overture and March from Act I, *Coffee, Tea, Bouffon*, and *Les Mirlitons* from the Act II *divertissement*, the Sugar-plum Fairy's variation, and the *Waltz of the Flowers*. This suite is as well known as the rest of the music in the ballet is unfamiliar.

As a whole, the ballet is not so successful as *Swan Lake* or *The Sleeping Beauty*, despite the fact that most of the music is excellent. Among its faults are, first, that the heroine, Clara, who is supposed to be a little girl, cannot therefore be allowed any opportunities for pure dancing, and a ballet heroine who does no more than mime prettily is not very interesting. Secondly, Act I has plenty of incident, but not of incidents that are particularly suitable for dancing, and the snow scene is, musically, too long. Thirdly, Act II has no dramatic interest whatever. Nevertheless, much of the music is brilliant, especially that for the *divertissement*, while the *pas de deux* is one of Tchaikovsky's noblest inventions. There is much, too, to admire in Act I; for instance, the music for the scene when Clara is alone in the dark room is scored with astonishing imagination, and the battle scene is extremely effective.

Chapter Six

STRAVINSKY AND THE DIAGHILEV BALLET

The Firebird   Petrushka

Serge Diaghilev (1872-1929) was a Russian impresario. Though Russian ballet, then as now, was probably the best in the world, Diaghilev found conservatism so strong in St Petersburg that there seemed no room there for his own somewhat revolutionary ideas. So he formed a company for the express purpose of giving ballet in Western Europe, and this company appeared in Paris from 1909 until the First World War, and in London from 1911. It would be impossible to exaggerate the effect Diaghilev's company had on music and culture generally, quite apart from ballet. Before his day ignorance of Russian music (apart from orchestral works by Tchaikovsky) and dancing standards was accepted as normal in Britain and France. Few intelligent people took ballet seriously or saw any future in it. The fact that all over the world to-day children learn ballet by the thousand, whereas in 1900 they did so by the dozen (if they did so at all), is due to Diaghilev more than to anyone else.

Ballet was neither his first nor his only interest. It was Diaghilev who brought Chaliapin's *Boris Godunov* to Paris in 1908, and at one time he ran an art review. He was in fact interested in all the arts, though he himself excelled in none of them. But artistic ability is not called for in an impresario. Diaghilev had the virtues that mattered. He was first and foremost an enthusiast and a fighter, and he had a nose for talent. He was the first man in the ballet world who wanted the best—not only in dancing, not only in music, but also in costumes and scenery. He employed established painters for his back-cloths: Picasso for *The Three-cornered Hat*, Derain for *La Boutique Fantasque*. These ballets came quite late in his career. At first he relied, as was natural, on fellow-Russians. The all-round talent he had collected for his first Paris season in 1909 was fabulous. Let me list a few great names:

Dancers: Pavlova, Karsavina, Nijinsky.
Choreographer: Michael Fokine.
Composer: Stravinsky.
Designers: Bakst, Benois.

Bakst and Benois had been friends of Diaghilev for ten years or more and had helped to form his tastes. None of the people in the above list (except Pavlova, who soon left the company) was famous when Diaghilev brought his company to Paris. It takes a great impresario to choose the best people from among the little known.

They did not rely on the repertoire of the past. Apart from a short-lived attempt at *Giselle*, all the ballets in their repertoire for the first ten years or so were new ones. Fokine, the company's choreographer, worked in two different directions. He devised choreography to well-known music of the past which was not originally intended for dancing, such as Rimsky-Korsakov's *Scheherazade* and Weber's *Invitation to the Dance* (this ballet was known as *La Spectre de la Rose*), and he had piano pieces orchestrated by the company's composers and then made ballets of them—hence *Les Sylphides*, to music by Chopin, and *Carnaval*, to music by Schumann. This type of ballet had not previously been attempted on any scale.

But Diaghilev was aware that the ideal was to have *new* music, composer and choreographer devising the ballet together. *The Firebird* (1910) was the first ballet entirely created from inside the company; Stravinsky wrote the music to Fokine's choreography, and the following year they had a similar success with *Petrushka*, for which the décor was by Benois. Karsarvina danced in both premières, and Nijinsky was the original Petrushka.

The presence of Nijinsky in the company had a big influence on Fokine's choreography and on the history of ballet generally. He was by all accounts the greatest male dancer within living memory. The male dancer had had a thin time in the nineteenth century; there was, for instance, no dance for a man in the first performance of *Coppélia*, and extremely little male dancing in *Giselle*. In Tchaikovsky's ballets there is still a very strong bias in favour of the girls. Both Fokine and Diaghilev were disposed to allow the male dancer more opportunities, but their enthusiasm for this point of view must have been very greatly increased by the presence in the company of a male dancer of unquestioned genius. It is hard to realize to-day how strange it seemed in 1912 to see a ballet like *L'Après-midi d'un Faune*, in which a man was the central figure. Diaghilev also countenanced a good deal of what is rather strangely called Greek dancing—that is, bare-foot dancing in simple, flowing robes—and when the girls are not allowed to dance on their points they tend to lose their apparent domination over the men. Generally, the ballets of this century have allotted the male dancer equal or almost equal importance with the female, and this is primarily due to Fokine and Nijinsky.

Diaghilev commissioned his ballets from the best composers, and in the years 1909-14 the best composers tended to write very difficult music for very large orchestras. One result of this was that full scores of all important ballets were printed as a matter of course. No one would care to conduct *Petrushka* or *The Rite of Spring* from a first violin part. Thus, whereas with nineteenth-century ballets full scores tend to be non-existent or only obtainable with great difficulty, while piano arrangements are fairly common, with twentieth-century ballets it is the piano arrangements that are the rarity, and the full scores the commonplace.

Diaghilev also started the practice of presenting three short ballets each evening. Most of his ballets last about half an hour, and scarcely any more than forty-five or fifty minutes. He did not think that audiences in Western Europe would sit through long three-act ballets as they did in Russia, and, as we have seen, his solitary experiment with the full-length ballet (the 1921 London production of *The Sleeping Princess*, as he called it) only confirmed him in this opinion.

The Firebird (*L'Oiseau de Feu*)

Scores. The full score of the complete ballet was published by the Russian publisher Jurgenson, and is not easily obtainable to-day. In 1919 Stravinsky arranged a suite from the ballet for concert purposes, cutting out many of the instruments for which he had originally written so that the suite could be played by normal-sized orchestras. The miniature score of this suite is published by Chester; it contains about half the ballet.
Recording. There are many recordings of the suite, but only one of the complete ballet: Decca LXT 5115, conducted by Stravinsky's life-long friend, Ernest Ansermet.

Igor Stravinsky, who was born near St Petersburg in 1882, studied composition with Rimsky-Korsakov. After his meeting with Diaghilev he began to spend most of his working life in Paris, and he did not return to Russia after the end of the First World War. Later he lived in Switzerland, and then in America. We are not here concerned with his numerous and surprising changes of style, which can only be paralleled in the work of his friend, Picasso. For our purposes all that matters is his style in his youth. He would now perhaps disdain the rich orchestration and grand ideas of his early ballets—the two dealt with in this chapter and his ultimate extravagance, *The Rite of Spring* (1913)—but the fact remains that he has never had another comparable success in the field of ballet, despite his numerous triumphs elsewhere. Of all ballets ever written, *The Rite of Spring* (or *Le Sacre du Printemps*, to give it its correct title) was written for the largest orchestra and made the loudest noise. As is well known, it caused a riot in the theatre on the first night. In the concert-hall we are now used to the noise and like it, but the work never seems to have been given as a ballet in this country and has not been in the repertoire of any company for very many years. Stravinsky has never since attempted the shattering effects to be found in this music; it was the end of a period in his career, and he next turned to small-scale works, written for a mere handful of instruments.

Just as *The Rite of Spring* comes at the end of Stravinsky's first period, so *The Firebird* comes at the beginning. It was first performed in June 1910 at the Paris Opéra. Prince Ivan and the Beautiful Tsarevna were danced by Fokine himself and his wife, Vera Fokina; Köstchei (the villain) by Cecchetti, and the Firebird, stupendously, by Karsavina. Besides devising the choreography and taking a leading part, Fokine made up the story. He was a good dancer, though he scarcely needed to be on this occasion, for *The Firebird* is old-fashioned in its relegation of the male dancer to subordinate rôles; the reforms were yet to come. But the mixture of Greek dancing by the Princesses and classical dancing by the Firebird must have seemed strange in its day. The scenery and costumes were devised by Golovine.

Faced with a vaguely Oriental subject, Stravinsky borrowed from the paint-box of his master, Rimsky-Korsakov, who had been engaged on a somewhat similar theme, the opera *Le Coq d'Or*, while Stravinsky was having lessons with him. The score calls for sixteen woodwind (double the usual number), a fairly modest brass section (except that at the very end Stravinsky asks for seven extra brass players on stage; it would be surprising if he had ever been allowed them), all the percussion instruments in use at that time, celeste, piano, three harps, and sixty string players. Few theatre pits can accommodate such an orchestra.

The music is constructed with astonishing skill, a great part of it from a tiny four-note phrase, which must occur thousands of times in the course of the ballet; nevertheless, it is quite easy to see the ballet several times without noticing it at all. One certainly notices its effect, for it is this phrase that gives the music its exotic atmosphere. Chromaticism had long been a standard Russian device for conveying exoticism, and the Firebird has musical affinities with the Queen of Shemakhan in *Le Coq d'Or*. In brief, Stravinsky takes three notes of the chromatic scale and adds a leap of a third. The phrase can go up and down, backward or forward, and thus has certain elements of what is now known as serial technique. Here are some examples:

A1 occurs at the Firebird's first entrance; it will be seen that in three bars the phrase comes in ascending form six times and in descending form once. A2 shows a sequence of descending phrases cutting across the bar rhythm, which makes them harder to hear. A3 is an example of a much repeated figure designed to suggest the fluttering of the Firebird's wings. A4 comes in the middle of a long tune and shows the phrase first descending and then immediately reversed, next ascending and then immediately reversed; thus these two bars contain the phrase in all its four possible shapes. A5 contains the phrase in its two commonest forms alternately, but overlapping; this is the only example so far given that is at all easy to spot with the ears, as opposed to the eyes. It will perhaps be a relief to learn that the above are among the harder examples; there are easier to come.

The music opens with a sombre, mysterious introduction based on

B1 is based on one of the less common forms of the phrase discussed above (see the end of A4). B2 represents Köstchei; Stravinsky frequently writes this chord sequence in a very quick tempo, which makes it, for me, unrecognizable. Just after the curtain goes up (just *before*, at Covent Garden) there occurs one of the few easily memorable tunes in the earlier part of the ballet.

This too seems to be associated with Köstchei, and it is his magic garden that we see when the curtain rises, though in fact it is so dark that we see very little. Across the stage flutters the brilliantly coloured Firebird (A1); for a moment the music swells in wonder, the stage empty, and then the Firebird flutters back (A2), pursued by Prince Ivan, wandering he knows not where. He catches her, and they converse. (Ivan is nearly always represented by a horn playing simple, diatonic melodies faintly suggestive of Russian folk-songs.) The Firebird warns him of the dangers of the garden (B2) and flutters on (A3). Again he catches her, and again they converse. This time Ivan's share of the dialogue is given to the oboe; it is quoted here to show the style of his tunes, none of which is ever repeated.

Now comes the *Firebird's Dance*, during which she flutters round a beautiful tree laden with golden apples and tries to pluck one of them. This dance is of considerable length, and A occurs in it a myriad times, though seldom easily recognizable. At length Ivan catches the Firebird in more determined fashion (a high viola solo akin to A2), and immediately her *Dance of Supplication* begins, as she begs for her release. He agrees to let her go if she will give him one of her feathers as an emblem of protection in these dangerous parts. Eventually she tears one out (A, very clear, rising on the trumpets) and gives it to him (A5); then she flies away (A, quickly descending and ascending on the clarinets several times). Ivan is now alone in the garden (a diatonic horn tune), but its menacing quality is suggested by C, still on the bassoons. The light grows stronger, and he becomes aware of a great gate leading into a castle. He hides when thirteen beautiful, white-clad, bare-footed princesses come from the castle. They have two short tunes.

The princesses pluck apples from the tree and play, throwing them one to another.

They have yet another and sadder tune, for they are held captive by the wicked Köstchei.

E2 also recurs about this time. The game breaks off suddenly and dramatically as the chief Princess, the beautiful Tsarevna, suddenly finds herself face to face with Ivan. He tries to reassure the princesses (horn solos) as they draw back frightened, but Ivan and the Tsarevna are compellingly drawn to each other. In the *Round Dance of the Princesses* six of the princesses encircle Ivan and six the Tsarevna, frustrating their attempts to get nearer to each other. While this is going on the orchestra rather pointedly plays a tune based on a folk-song (No. 79 in Rimsky-Korsakov's collection) all about a dandified young man who was so vain that his girl could not bring herself to marry him.

It is the first two bars of this that are taken from the folk-song. Soon there is another tune.

Both tunes recur, and at the climax of the second appearance of J Ivan and the Tsarevna get near enough to kiss. The music quietens down, and, as day dawns (the second side of the Decca record begins at this point), the princesses steal back to the castle. Ivan, after a few moments alone, takes courage and to a loud pizzicato chord (with B2 on the brass) flings open the gates. Immediately bells sound, and Köstchei's monsters appear on all sides; the music is at first a jumble of sound. When the noise dies away Köstchei himself, old and evil, comes out of his castle (bassoons play B2 slowly and clearly). He beckons to Ivan with long, taloned fingers (C). The music rises to a sudden hubbub as Ivan tries to escape, without avail. The princesses come from the castle and plead for him (E1), but Köstchei relentlessly embarks on one of his terrible spells (trombone chords and rumbles on the drums), aiming to turn Ivan to stone. The spell is beginning to take effect on him when, just in time, he waves the feather given him by the Firebird, and her arrival (with A fluttering up and down on instrument after instrument) is unmistakable. She too has magic powers, and all Köstchei's monsters (though not Köstchei) are soon dancing in spite of themselves.

In this *Danse Infernale* the music shows when the Firebird is asserting her powers,

and when the princesses are weeping at the uncertain situation (G, or something very like it). The dance grows wilder, until with a crash all the creatures fall flat on the ground. The Firebird then charms them to sleep with a lovely tune (note the marked phrases).

By the end Köstchei too is asleep (B2 on the bassoons). Ivan rushes into the castle and comes out with a great egg, Köstchei's soul. To short, rising flourishes on the orchestra he raises it above his head, and as he dashes it to the ground (gong crash) he destroys Köstchei for ever. Immediately a great darkness pervades everything.

In the short final scene all is light. The castle has vanished, and a great city is spread out on the back-cloth. All the unfortunates whom Köstchei had turned to stone become alive again and join in the general thanksgiving. There is no dancing; the scene gradually builds up into a great tableau, while the orchestra repeats louder and louder another Russian folk-song from the Rimsky-Korsakov collection (No. 21).

There is a momentary interruption to this as the Firebird appears and places the Tsarevna's hand in Ivan's (A5 quietly on the violins). Then N returns, quicker and in a new rhythm (N2), and the ballet ends to glorious music.

Petrushka

Score. The miniature score of the whole ballet is published by Boosey & Hawkes.
Recording. Of the several recordings Decca LXT 5375, conducted by Ansermet, is still the best.

Petrushka was first performed in June 1911 in Paris. It is described as a burlesque in four scenes; the story was put together by Stravinsky and Benois, the latter being responsible for the scenery and costumes, and the choreography was Fokine's. Petrushka and the Ballerina were danced by Nijinsky and Karsavina, the Showman by Cecchetti. The music is written for a somewhat more modest orchestra than *The Firebird*, and it plays for about thirty-five minutes.

FIRST PART: THE SHROVE-TIDE FAIR

The scene is the Admiralty Square in St Petersburg in 1830 at carnival time. The square is full of people, side-shows, cheap-jacks, merry-go-rounds, and all the fun of the fair. The first tune we hear clearly is one of the many folk-songs Stravinsky has introduced into his score; it may be of interest if we give these (where they occur) with a rough translation of a verse or two of the original words. This one is No. 47 in Rimsky-Korsakov's collection.

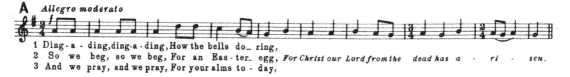

A distraction is provided by a street dancer, who spreads out a little carpet and pirouettes on it, accompanied by a barrel-organ.

(This is a music-hall ditty which Stravinsky heard played on a barrel-organ when he was in the south of France.) For the repeat the barrel-organist plays a trumpet. Soon we hear a maudlin tune on the cracked barrel-organ (represented by the clarinets, with occasional notes left out as though the works had gone wrong), with a rival musical box playing at the same time, while rival dancers strive for the attention of the crowd. There is a great deal more bustling and jostling (A), and then two uniformed drummers persuade the crowd into a sudden silence, in preparation for a performance on the little stage at the back. To mysterious music the old Showman comes forward. He plays an old-fashioned, sentimental solo on his flute and then draws the curtains of the little stage, thus revealing three puppets: a Blackamoor, a Ballerina, and Petrushka himself, a floppy, pathetic creature. The Showman touches each in turn with his flute, and they break into a wild *Russian Dance*, using only their legs; their bodies remain rigid.

The Blackamoor, the Ballerina, and Petrushka

(The music of this dance has a concertante piano part and was composed before the ballet was first thought of.) Such is the Showman's magic that the three puppets soon step down from the little stage and continue their dance among the crowd—the Moor strong and insensitive, the Ballerina with red painted cheeks like a doll, and Petrushka a sad, self-distrustful clown, his bones in the wrong place, like those of a spastic child.

Second Part: Petrushka

Throughout this ballet a roll on the side-drum joins each scene to the next, filling the time while the curtain is down. When the curtain rises we see Petrushka's room at the back of the little theatre. The show is over, and as the scene starts he is flung in by the Showman to lie crumpled on the floor, no longer wanted. The music of this scene, with its difficult piano solo, resembles a piano concerto. We must pause here for a moment to introduce Petrushka's leitmotivs, which have not so far been heard in the ballet. They are very short.

The second line of the above occurs when Petrushka flies into a sudden rage at the sight of the Showman's portrait hanging on the wall, the only sign of furnishing in the whole miserable room. Soon two demure bars on the piano (solo) usher in the Ballerina.

Petrushka, who adores her, immediately indulges in silly antics, leaping about in front of her like an unpleasant small boy showing off. (The orchestra takes up the three repeated notes that start and end E.) The Ballerina runs frightened from the room (high clarinet cadenza). At first mortified, Petrushka is soon filled with a sense of the tragic futility of his existence and beats his fists on the wall in crazy attempts to get out (D1, 2, and 3). But when his fist finally goes right through the wall all he hears is the squeejee music of the fairground; there is nowhere to escape to. With a defiant trumpet call the scene ends.

THIRD PART: THE BLACKAMOOR

The Blackamoor's room at least has a couch in it, and the Blackamoor himself is lying on it, face upward, tossing a coconut up in the air and catching it. He is a silly fellow. His tune is accompanied by African rhythms on the bass drum and cymbals.

The Ballerina comes in, very jauntily playing a trumpet, and then dances some old-time waltzes for the Moor's entertainment; both the main tunes are by Joseph Lanner, who, with the elder Strauss, established the waltz as a popular favourite in Vienna at about the time that the story of *Petrushka* is supposed to have happened.

(G1 is from the *Steyrische Tänze*, Op. 165; D2 from *Die Schönbrunner*, Op. 200.) When the Moor tries clumsily to join in the waltz F is combined with G2. Both waltz tunes are repeated several times. The Moor is much enjoying himself; he has actually got the Ballerina on his knee when Petrushka is heard outside (D1, 2, and 3). Petrushka bursts in, feebly threatening the Moor, who is soon chasing him round and round the room—and eventually right out of it. As the curtain comes down the Ballerina is again on the Moor's knee.

The Ballerina enters the Blackamoor's Room

FOURTH PART: THE SHROVE-TIDE FAIR AND THE DEATH OF PETRUSHKA

We are back on the fairground. The greater part of this final scene is, in effect, a *divertissement* danced by various sections of the crowd. A group of nursemaids dance to a folk-tune called *I was at a Feast*.[1]

Subsequent verses reveal that the person supposed to be singing the song is a woman. That, of course, is why Stravinsky chose this tune for the nursemaids. Later the nursemaids have another folk-song to dance to.

H and J are ingeniously combined.

A peasant leads in a dancing bear on a chain; the tuba represents the creature's pathetic attempts to dance, and the clarinet his master's piping, which has an Asiatic flavour.

Two gipsy girls of questionable morals dance with a drunken, jovial businessman.

Now a group of coachmen dance to another folk-tune, *I was going up a Hill*.[2]

[1] This was used by Balakirev in his *Overture on Three Russian Themes* ; it also comes in Tchaikovsky's collection of folk-songs arranged for piano duet, but this gives no words. It is given here as it appears in Filippov's set of forty folk-songs harmonized by Rimsky-Korsakov (No. 39); it does not come in Rimsky-Korsakov's better known collection.

[2] This comes in Tchaikovsky's collection of folk-songs with words, which was unknown until its recent publication in Russia as part of his complete works.

Soon the nursemaids are dancing with the coachmen (H), and during a climax L appears in canon between the brass and the violins. Masqueraders appear in fantastic clothes, some dressed like devils, others like animals, and, as darkness draws on, the crowd is caught up in the general dancing (A again, from the First Part).

Suddenly all the noise and tumult is hushed, a high trumpet note falls into the tail-end of D3 (repeated complete by the cor anglais), and uneasy sounds are heard from behind the curtain of the little stage. All gaze in wonder at the billowing curtain until Petrushka comes running from behind it, pursued by the angry Moor (D1). To quick repetitions of D3 the Moor strikes him down with his scimitar, and there is complete silence. As Petrushka writhes in his death agonies we hear D3, sounding inexpressibly pathetic as it is played very slowly by the clarinet and then by a solo violin. An officious policeman trots off to fetch the Showman, who comes in to the mysterious music associated with him in the First Part, pushes his way through the crowd thronging round the body, holds up Petrushka's remains, and shows every one that he was only a puppet, stuffed with sawdust. The crowd, only half believing, disperses slowly in the gathering darkness until only the Showman is left in the square, the limp puppet dangling from his hands. And then, over the top of the theatre, appears Petrushka's ghost, his fists raised as he curses his master (D1 and 2 on muted trumpet), and the curtain comes down. Was he a puppet, or was there some breath of life in him?

Musically, *Petrushka* is a much stronger ballet than *The Firebird*. It wears well in the concert hall, whereas much of *The Firebird*, if it was played complete, would pall without the dancing. The music is more broadly conceived, less finicky, and less derivative; the score of *Petrushka* is in fact a miracle of originality. Nevertheless, it is possible to prefer *The Firebird* as a ballet; it is certainly an easier work to bring off. The long crowd scenes in *Petrushka* are desperately difficult. They need very complex production, with numerous tiny character studies; otherwise the visual interest will flag. Ballet-dancers, being young, naturally lack experience in portraying the middle-aged and elderly in mime. Furthermore, the tilt in favour of the male dancer is here almost too strong. The Ballerina has few opportunities, and in any case is not a very sympathetic character. The glories of *Petrushka* are first the music, and secondly the title part, one of the most dramatic male rôles in all ballet.

Chapter Seven

SOME MODERN BALLETS

Daphnis and Chloe   Job   The Prince of the Pagodas

When Diaghilev became established in Paris it was natural that he should seek the collaboration of composers and artists in Western Europe, and the following ballets were among the results:

Daphnis and Chloe (1912). Music by Ravel; book and choreography by Fokine; scenery and costumes by Bakst. Nijinsky and Karsavina danced the title-rôles.

Jeux (1913). Music by Debussy; book and choreography (largely about tennis) by Nijinsky; scenery by Bakst.

The Legend of Joseph (1914). Music by Richard Strauss; book by Hugo von Hofmannsthal and Count Harry Kessler; choreography by Fokine; costumes by Bakst. Leonid Massine made his début as a dancer in the title-rôle.

La Boutique Fantasque (1919). Music by Rossini (arranged by Respighi); choreography by Massine; curtain, settings, and costumes by Derain.

The Three-cornered Hat (1919). Music by Falla; book by Martinez Sierra; choreography by Massine; scenery and costumes by Picasso.

The Prodigal Son (1929). Music by Prokofiev; choreography by Balanchine. Décor by Renault. Lifar took the title-rôle, and Dolin also had an important part.

It is curious that the first three, all of them ambitious works, all failed. Perhaps Fokine and Nijinsky found it harder to collaborate with foreign composers than with Russian; certainly Fokine and Ravel seldom saw eye to eye. The War made things desperately difficult for the company, and any new work on a large scale was out of the question. After 1918 things were never quite the same. For one thing Nijinsky was no longer with the company, having been driven out of his senses in the war years. Furthermore, Fokine had left the company, while Stravinsky, now a composer with a world-wide reputation, was only intermittently available. In fact, it was virtually a new company, and the only member of it who could be spoken of in the same breath as the pre-war figures was Massine.

Massine could never equal Nijinsky as a serious dancer, but in comedy rôles he excelled him, while as a choreographer he was in the very highest class. After Diaghilev died in 1929 the company was kept going for some years by Colonel de Basil, but eventually Massine broke away and tried his hand at running his own company. Latterly he had been spending his talents, perhaps unwisely, in devising ballets to symphonies. Tchaikovsky's Fifth (*Les Présages*) and Brahms's Fourth (*Choreartium*) were dubious successes, Beethoven's Seventh a deplorable failure; only the imaginative steps he devised for Berlioz's *Symphonie Fantastique* might bear reviving to-day. But his light comedy ballets—*La Boutique Fantasque*, *The Three-cornered Hat*, and *Le Beau Danube* (to music by Johann Strauss)—must still have a future. Generally speaking, Massine showed too little interest in devising ballets to specially written music (though one remembers with pleasure his Hindemith ballets). His astonishing ability for finding movements for any and every piece of music half-an-hour long has led to numerous less talented hands trying to do the same, with the result that there are now very few works of suitable length that have *not* been made into ballets.

Russian Ballet, as understood in Western Europe, declined steadily between the wars as the supply of exiles grew less numerous, and there is now no prospect of its revival—nor, indeed, very much need, for alongside this decline there has been a renaissance of ballet in England and, more recently, in America. I have no intention of telling here the story of the Royal Ballet at Covent Garden, from its beginnings at Sadler's Wells Theatre in 1931 to the present day. Its chief contribution has been the revival of the great nineteenth-century ballets described earlier in this book, and in this it has been supported by the now defunct International Ballet and by the Festival Ballet. So healthy is the position to-day that British dancers are now much in demand on the Continent as teachers—for instance, in Germany, where it is admitted that standards are much lower than in England.

But one cannot point to many great ballets devised to new music in the Royal Ballet's repertoire. *Checkmate*, with music by Arthur Bliss, was a landmark before the Second World War, but it is sad that we had to wait till 1957 for Benjamin Britten's first ballet, and that the company has yet to sponsor a new ballet with music by William Walton. Perhaps it is not for want of trying. At least, there are increasing signs that young composers are being given their chance. Decisions must be hard to make when commissioning a new work. History shows that ballets with good music are far more likely to succeed than ballets with poor music.

I wish that I could discuss here Constant Lambert's *Tiresias*—a fine work, musically— but it is no longer in the repertoire, and no recordings exist. Similarly, an insufficiency of recordings prevents my including the full-length Prokofiev ballets *Cinderella* and *Romeo and Juliet*. It should be remembered that in Russia there has never been a bias against the single work which fills the whole evening. Before the First World War Glazunov to some extent succeeded Tchaikovsky as a purveyor of the three-act ballet, and since about 1930 (only then was it possible to put ballet on a sound footing after the ravages of the Revolution) a considerable number of long ballets have been written in Russia by such composers as Asafiev, whose *Fountains of Bakhchisserai* is still very popular. But, Prokofiev apart, their music seems insufficiently interesting to be worth exporting outside Russia.

To guard myself against accusations of criminal omission, I must stress here that I am mainly concerned in this book with the Music of the Best Ballets, and that my admittedly superficial historical interludes are intended for beginners only, who will, I hope, pass on to more learned works (in which they will find the music ignored).

Daphnis and Chloe
(RAVEL)

Scores. Durand publish a full score of the whole ballet, and also of two suites, called ' First Series ' and ' Second Series.' These are not suites in the usual sense of the word, but uninterrupted sequences from the ballet. The second, which consists of the last fifteen minutes or so, is much the more often played in the concert hall, because it can be performed without a chorus. All these scores can be obtained from United Music Publishers.
Recordings. There are many recordings of the First and Second Series, and three of the whole ballet. There is still much to be said for the oldest of these: Decca LXT 2775. H.M.V. ALP 1374 is also good.

The Covent Garden production of *Daphnis and Chloe* makes no attempt to reproduce Fokine's original choreography. It is very doubtful if there is anyone alive who remembers it, but, as Fokine's version failed, and Frederick Ashton's is highly successful, no one has cause for regret. The score contains enough information about the action to ensure that much the same things happen at much the same moments in the music. Nor are Bakst's designs used at Covent Garden; the décor and costumes are by John Craxton.

Daphnis and Chloe is written for a very large orchestra and hidden chorus and it contains some of the loveliest music to be heard in any ballet. It is, however, very atmospheric music, almost entirely lacking in strong, easily memorized tunes such as are found in *Petrushka*. A study of the music reveals an elaborate leitmotiv system, but one would have to see this ballet many times before becoming aware of this through the ears alone.

The story of *Daphnis and Chloe* is taken from the Latin poet, Longus. There are three scenes, and the ballet plays for over fifty minutes. There is no orchestral prelude, the curtain rising almost at once.

SCENE I

It is a spring afternoon in a classical landscape; at the back is a grotto, and three statues of nymphs. I quote the music heard as the curtain rises; these bars contain the germs from which a great deal of the music springs.

Daphnis and Chloe

A1 is no more than a swaying between adjacent notes, A2 represents the nymphs, and A3 is Daphnis himself. All these tunes recur frequently. At first the stage is empty, but when the music quickens to a climax (A2 on the trumpets) shepherds and shepherdesses arrive with gifts for the nymphs of Pan. There follows the *Danse Religieuse*, based on three cool, fragmentary tunes.

The wordless chorus join in with A1. The dancers break off when Daphnis is seen passing with his sheep at the back (A3 on the oboe). Chloe follows him (A3 on the flute); they go from our sight, and the *Danse Religieuse* is resumed with the themes combined—*e.g.*, B1 and 3 at the climax. Daphnis and Chloe return (A3), and again the dance is interrupted (A1 and 2 on the voices and solo violin).

A new dance begins in quick seven-four time, with the girls surrounding Daphnis.

Again the themes are fragmentary. Chloe is a little jealous, until the men start paying attention to her and put such thoughts out of her mind.

C2 returns, and also C1, and in a *Danse Générale* all the tunes in C and D are woven together in counterpoint of astonishing complexity. One of the peasants, Dorkon, is especially enamoured of Chloe and tries to kiss her. Daphnis strikes him and is very tender with Chloe.

Note the falling fifth at the start, characteristic of Daphnis's tune. To repetitions of E it is suggested that Dorkon and Daphnis shall compete at dancing, a kiss from Chloe being the prize.

Dorkon's dance is grotesque; it starts with uncouth noises on the bassoons and ends with an imitation of the general laughter he causes. Then, after a brief interlude (E2), we hear Daphnis's dance, slow and graceful.

To the tender music of E Daphnis is told to claim his prize. Dorkon tries to intervene but is chased away amid more laughter, and then, after a silent bar, Daphnis and Chloe embrace each other to a quiet but ecstatic version of A3. The crowd go, taking Chloe with them, and Daphnis is left to meditate on his own (A1 on the voices).

Lykanion, a young married girl, finds him (clarinet flourishes in thirds). She dances provocatively before him but is coolly received (F on the horns, very quietly). Her advances are interrupted by the sound of fighting; tangled in the orchestral web is the pirate theme (G1) on muted horns.

Daphnis, worrying about Chloe (A3 loud), hurries away, and Chloe, terrified, comes in from another direction (E). There is a quick climax with G2 on the trumpets; the pirates have found her and carried her off. The music is suddenly hushed; Daphnis, returning

F

(A3 quietly on the violas), finds the sandal she has dropped and, suddenly despairing (A2 on the full orchestra), curses the gods and falls to the ground in a swoon (A3, finally on the bass clarinet).

The three nymphs descend one by one from their pedestals. (A2 on flute, horn, and clarinet in turn). They begin a slow, mysterious dance in which A1 and 2 are prominent. Finding Daphnis (A3), they invoke the help of Pan, who appears and sends Daphnis, now recovered, in search of his beloved.

There follows an *Interlude* in which unaccompanied voices sadly meditate on A1, until interrupted by the pirates' horn and trumpet calls (G2).

SCENE 2

The scene is the pirates' camp at night, lit by torches. A vigorous *Pirates' Dance* starts the scene; when the music quietens down a new tune is heard.

A1 is very prominent in the accompaniment. This is a long dance, with H recurring a great many times, and G often apparent at climaxes.

When it is over Bryaxis, the pirate chief, has Chloe brought before him (E) and orders her to dance. She does so, the falling fifths of Daphnis's tune suggesting her thoughts. As the music rises to its second climax Bryaxis lustfully seizes her, but suddenly the great waves of sound cease, and the atmosphere becomes charged with mystery; lights flicker, satyrs leap in the shadows, and great Pan himself is seen outlined against the mountains as the music rises to a new climax. The pirates flee in terror.

SCENE 3

All at first is dark. Slowly the spring morning dawns to the sound of innumerable rivulets (we have now reached the start of the frequently played 'Second Series'). The rising dawn theme has affinities with that of Daphnis.

Soon we hear the only long tune in the whole ballet, and a most beautiful tune it is.

As daylight brightens we see Daphnis lying before the nymphs' shrine. A shepherd passes, blowing his pipe, and momentarily interrupts a repetition of K. At the climax shepherds find Daphnis and bring Chloe to him, and they embrace to another ecstatic version of A3. The music quietens down, and Daphnis is told that Pan has saved Chloe.

To the music of a long flute solo Daphnis and Chloe mime the tale of Pan and Syrinx. At the end of this there is more embracing (A3), the lovers offer a sacrifice before the nymphs' shrine (A1 on strings and woodwind against A2 on the trumpets), and every one breaks into an immensely energetic *Danse Générale*. This is a long piece, requiring virtuoso playing from the orchestra, and it contains the most exhilarating music Ravel ever wrote. The tunes are too quick for quotation, and there is very little reference back to earlier tunes, though we may suppose that when E occurs on the violins Daphnis and Chloe are momentarily prominent in the dancing.

Job
(VAUGHAN WILLIAMS)

Scores. A miniature score and a piano arrangement of the whole ballet are published by the Oxford University Press.
Recording. Decca LXT 2937, conducted by Sir Adrian Boult, to whom the music is dedicated.

Job, described as 'A Masque for Dancing,' received its first performance from the Camargo Society in London in 1931. The scenario is based on William Blake's illustrations to the *Book of Job*, and was devised by Geoffrey Keynes and the artist Gwendolen Raverat, who was responsible for the costumes and décor. The choreography was by Ninette de Valois, who at the time must have been busy on her plans for the new Sadler's Wells Ballet company, and the music was by Ralph Vaughan Williams. When the ballet is revived at Covent Garden décor by John Piper is used.

Before this work appeared Vaughan Williams had been going through a period when his music seemed almost spinelessly dependent on folk elements, and the tremendous strength and vitality of *Job* came as a surprise. It was in fact the herald of other dynamic works, such as the Fourth Symphony, and it is generally regarded as one of his most successful pieces. Of all ballets this one is perhaps the most dependent on its music. Much of the dancing is not and cannot be very interesting. Tableaux suggesting Blake's rather uncouth drawings, interspersed with slow, stately Greek dancing, could hardly make the ballet visually exciting, one would think. But it has been many people's experience that this magnificent music, coupled to one of the most tremendous and searing of Biblical stories, can produce a most moving entertainment. But the music must come first; unless more attention than usual is given to it the ballet will not make much impression.

I must not exaggerate the lack of dancing in this work. Satan is a tremendous part, and no one who saw him will forget Robert Helpmann's performance of it. But his is the only part that gives a real chance to an ambitious dancer; there is certainly nothing here for ballerinas.

There are nine scenes in this masque, and throughout it is to be supposed that the front of the stage represents the Earth, and the steps rising at the back Heaven.

SCENE 1: INTRODUCTION
The first scene starts with music that suggests complete spiritual peace.

We see Job sitting with his wife and servants; shepherds and husbandmen cross the stage and salute him. The marked phrase in A is developed, and at the end (B1) there are hints of the dance that follows.

This nine-eight dance (B2) is for Job's sons and daughters. There is a short middle section for the woodwind alone. As Job stands and blesses his children B2 is joined by a broad descending tune on the strings.

Satan before God (Scene I)

When all except Job and his wife have gone Satan appears. He is dressed only in a loincloth. He has three themes, of which we now hear two: C1, evil and prowling, and C2, defiant.

He appeals to God, and the Heavens are opened revealing "God sitting in majesty, surrounded by the Sons of God." "The line of Angels stretches from Earth to Heaven." We hear the rising fourths associated with the Godhead (D1) and the sublimely beautiful progression, D2.

These ideas seem implicit in the noble *Saraband of the Sons of God*, which now follows. When it is over God rises and beckons to Satan. A light falls on Job, sitting at the side of the stage (A). Satan cries, "Put forth Thy hand now and touch all that he hath and he will curse Thee to Thy face" (C1 and 2 alternating bar by bar, followed by C3). God says, "All that he hath is in thy power" (D3), and Satan goes. The Sons of God resume their saraband, and the scene ends.

SCENE 2: SATAN'S DANCE OF TRIUMPH

Heaven is empty, and God's throne vacant. In the introduction we hear C1 and 2, and then, when Satan's dance begins, there are new tunes of diabolical vigour, including

A trio section takes up an accompaniment figure that has been heard constantly in the dance (F1) and turns it into a new, and grossly evil, tune (F2). Both have affinities with C3.

The opening section returns, and there is a ghastly parody of the plainsong Gloria ("Glory to God in the highest") as Satan kneels before the empty throne in mock adoration.

To the music of F1 the hosts of Hell come scurrying in, and, to a triumphant version of C3 on the full orchestra, Satan sits on God's throne. The scene ends with a sudden black-out.

SCENE 3: MINUET OF THE SONS OF JOB AND THEIR WIVES

Satan enters suddenly (C2), and the dancers fall dead.

SCENE 4: JOB'S DREAM

We hear first a solemn fugato on this tune, for strings alone.

Job is seen asleep. At the first climax Satan enters to a chromatically descending theme perhaps deriving from C3. He "stands over Job and calls up terrifying visions of Plague, Pestilence, Famine, Battle, Murder and Sudden Death who posture before Job." K represents "Battle, etc."

Satan and the dancers stand round Job, gloating (C2).

SCENE 5: DANCE OF THE THREE MESSENGERS

The funeral cortège of Job's sons and daughters passes. Job still blesses God (J).

SCENE 6: DANCE OF JOB'S COMFORTERS

Satan introduces "three wily hypocrites" into Job's presence (C1). Their tune sounds the more hypocritical for being given to the saxophone.

Their pretended sympathy turns suddenly to anger and reproach, and their true value is shown by the suggestion of C3 in their 'anger' motive.

After a return of the hypocritical music Job stands and curses God, and here too Satan is behind the music.

Heaven slowly lights up, and Satan is seen enthroned, surrounded by the creatures of Hell (C3). Job cowers in terror.

SCENE 7: ELIHU'S DANCE OF YOUTH AND BEAUTY

A violin solo, with a clarinet tune for middle section. This leads into the *Pavane of the Sons of the Morning*. At first the figures are only dimly seen.

The violin theme in bar 4 is one of God's themes (D3), and as Heaven grows lighter the solemn dancers are seen to be before God's throne.

SCENE 8: GALLIARD OF THE SONS OF THE MORNING

Satan enters (C1, 2, and 3) and claims the victory over Job. God banishes him from Heaven (D3), and to the jubilant tune of the galliard the Sons of the Morning drive him down.

At the climax, when the tune is repeated for the last time, Satan "falls out of Heaven," as in one of Blake's pictures.

There follows an *Altar Dance*.

Young men and maidens on Earth build an altar and decorate it with flowers. Heaven is still visible rising behind them. Job blesses the altar (P on the woodwind against J on the strings). Dancing on both Earth and Heaven is seen (N, P, and J all at once). The scene ends with a majestic reference to D2.

SCENE 9: EPILOGUE

The music of the brief *Epilogue* is based on A. Job, an old and humbled man, sits with his wife while friends bring him presents. His three daughters enter, and he blesses them.

Job raises one insurmountable problem in the theatre (it would not be insurmountable if a little sense could be shown in high places). It is illegal to depict God on the stage. He is to be seen in stage performances of the medieval morality play, *Everyman*, to the advantage of all who see this sincere and spiritual work. *Job*, one would think, is equally sincere and spiritual. Nevertheless, in the theatre the Person high on the throne of Heaven has to be called, in the programme, 'Job's Spiritual Self,' which makes nonsense of the story to anyone in the audience who is unaware of Blake's and Vaughan Williams's intentions.

I feel myself that Elihu is a weakness in the ballet. It is quite impossible for the dancer to make clear who he is or what he is doing. The Covent Garden programme says, "by his dance he shows Job his true relation to the Universe, and Job realizes his complacent materialism." It would take a very remarkable dancer to convey all this.

Vaughan Williams is probably the only British composer of this century equipped to express both Satan's diablerie and the celestial sublimity of Heaven.

The Prince of the Pagodas

(BRITTEN)

Score. The piano arrangement will be published by Boosey & Hawkes.
Recording. The greater part of the music is on Decca LXT 5336-37, played by the Covent Garden Orchestra, conducted by the composer.

The Prince of the Pagodas is the first full-length ballet by an important British composer. It was first performed at Covent Garden on January 1, 1957, with choreography by John Cranko (who also wrote the scenario) and décor by John Piper. Benjamin Britten very sensibly spent a good deal of time studying the music of Tchaikovsky's ballets while at work on it; there are no better models. Perhaps Tchaikovsky's influence can be found in the *pas de six* in Act III and in Belle Rose's theme; also in the plan of the ballet, which spins out the plot with a *divertissement* of air, water, and fire dances at the beginning of Act II, and another on a larger scale in Act III. *The Sleeping Beauty* has similar *divertissements* in its second and third acts. It is curious that Cranko was also the choreographer of the dances deriving from the four elements of earth, air, fire, and water in Tippett's opera, *The Midsummer Marriage*, and these too may have influenced the *divertissement* in Act II of *The Prince of the Pagodas*.

The music of Britten's ballet is more consciously 'tuneful' than that of his recent operas, and though at first some of it may sound astringent to elderly listeners, there are many beauties that can be appreciated at once, or almost at once. This is by no means modern music for a small coterie 'in the know,' but modern music at its most approachable, meeting the listener half-way. It is scored for triple woodwind, and the only unusual instruments are a 'native drum' and a very small timpani; also there is a part for piano duet. For every character there is a theme, and the themes that belong to the important characters are memorable and, for the most part, easily recognizable; they show Britten's remarkable grasp of musical characterization. The Prince, the hero of the ballet, has two themes, one when he is in human form, and another, much less assertive, when he is disguised as a salamander. The heroine, Belle Rose, also has two themes, and so has her haughty sister, Belle Épine.

As may have been guessed, the story is the old one common to so many fairy tales of the beautiful younger sister who is bullied by her elder sister but gets her man in the end.

Belle Rose and the Salamander

ACT I: THE COURT OF THE EMPEROR OF THE MIDDLE KINGDOM

Before the curtain rises there is a short introduction based on a fanfare theme which recurs frequently throughout the ballet

and the hard-to-recognize salamander tune, rhythmically akin to the first famous theme in Beethoven's Fifth Symphony, only very much slower at this point.

The curtain goes up on the court of the old Emperor, though at first we see no one but the Fool and the Dwarf. The Fool is an endearing creature, amiable and slightly ridiculous. After some horseplay (to *glissandi* on the trombones) the 'court' enters to a short, piquant march (bassoon solo), and soon the vapid courtiers are dancing a cheerful, hair-brained gavotte round the doddering old Emperor.

The gavotte has a contrasting theme, vacillating between two adjacent notes;

this represents the Emperor himself, who does a little dancing too until exhaustion overcomes him. The saxophone is associated with him throughout the ballet. Fanfares announce the arrival, inevitable in ballets of this kind, of four kings, each hoping to find a wife at the Emperor's court. Their tune is full of courtesy and good breeding.

The kings then establish their identities in four short solo dances. First the King of the North, a vigorous man.

For the King of the East there is slow, mysterious music (distant muted horn), while the King of the West has a *pointilliste* cat-on-hot-bricks woodwind tune, which seems to be satirizing twelve-note music. The King of the South is accompanied by African drum rhythms and a fanfare ringing high on the horns.

The Dwarf is now sent scurrying off (clarinet runs) to fetch the Emperor's elder daughter, Belle Épine; her music emphasizes her arrogance.

She has another theme too, a long one, slowly rising over a persistent bass. After the kings have bowed to her (E) the Fool hurries off to fetch the younger daughter, Belle Rose, who is, of course, as sweet-tempered as she is beautiful. A high note on the oboe, slowly falling in decorative phrases to harp accompaniment, announces her arrival, and her second, and more important, tune follows at once, still on the oboe, a lovely, forlorn melody.

This is repeated by the strings while the oboe rambles sadly on above them. Fearful that she might accept one of the kings, those unseen benevolences that control the destinies of fairy-tale princesses now offer her a vision of worthier metal; from nowhere there springs a Prince.

In her imagination she dances with this wondrous creature while the orchestra plays three variations on his theme; the first two begin as follows:

In the third variation the tune is heard loud on the trombones in its original form. (Here I use the word 'variation' in its musical, as opposed to balletic, sense.) As the vision vanishes Belle Rose's forlorn oboe themes return (H). The kings, overcome by her beauty, kneel before her (E on the strings), but the Emperor angrily places his crown on Belle Épine's head (climax on the brass, followed by H), and Belle Rose, humiliated, runs from the room (rapid, descending scale-like phrase). The haughty Belle Épine now dances disdainfully and briefly with each king in turn: first the King of the North (F), then East, then West, then South, their tunes distorted by her insistent waltz rhythm. Finally she spurns them all, and they, angry at such treatment, forget their good manners (E "fast and furious" on the trumpets). The Emperor tries unsuccessfully to calm them (D), and soon Belle Rose returns to see what she can do (H). Almost at once there is an unexpected distraction; distant fanfares (A) herald the arrival of four frogs bringing a large emerald casket (climax, then E on the bassoons). Belle Épine tries to open it but cannot (G slow and pizzicato). But for Belle Rose it opens of its own accord (a swish on the celeste), and the courtiers laugh (C). The frogs, who share the courtly tune of the Kings (E), invite Belle Rose to step into a great golden net, which carries her high into the air and out of sight; the Prince's tune, loud on the trombones (J), tells us to whom she is being taken.

ACT II

Scene 1: Belle Rose's Strange Voyage to the Kingdom of the Pagodas
  The much repeated 'journey' tune contains more than a suggestion of the Prince.

On her journey Belle Rose passes through the elements of air, water, and fire (though not earth), and the creatures of these elements are given dance sequences on a considerable scale; these contain some of the loveliest music in the ballet. First the Clouds:

The Clouds are soon joined by the Stars, their music high in the register, and much later by the Moon (a cool, falling phrase on the trumpet, carried on as an arpeggio by the clarinet). The Clouds and Stars music is then heard together, and the Moon reappears (tubular bells). Next on her journey (L) Belle Rose finds herself among sea creatures of various kinds. We hear short, darting arpeggio figures swirling and coiling, and some unmistakable waves. This opening section is followed by a strong, vigorous 'Boys' variation' (*The Sea-horses*), for the trumpets (unfortunately cut on the record), a wonderfully watery 'Girls' variation' (*The Fish Creatures*, harp and clarinet prominent), and an energetic coda (more waves). Again Belle Rose journeys on (L), and the Fire dances that follow are similar in design to the Water dances. After the opening section, in which the trumpet depicts the tongues of flame licking ever upward, there is a variation (not on the record) for "male flame, roaring and burning," another for "female flame, flickering and fluttering," and a coda of great vigour, with fascinating cross-rhythms.

We also hear more flames licking upward on the trumpets and trombones.
  Thus both the Water and the Fire dances are constructed very like a Tchaikovsky *pas de deux:* Duet—'male' variation—'female' variation—coda for all.
  By now Belle Rose is tired (L much slower); her journey ended, she finds herself alone on the dark stage (H, much decorated, as a violin solo).

Scene 2: The Arrival and Adventures of Belle Rose in the Kingdom of the Pagodas

As the light grows stronger she sees "a jewelled palace made of pagodas," and now follows a brilliant imitation of the gamelan orchestras of Bali in the East Indies, in which cymbals, vibraphone, xylophone, glockenspiel, celeste, piano duet, gong, piccolo, and harp produce authentic-sounding, dry, fascinating clankings. The pagodas are tall, narrow structures; there are several on the stage, and they unexpectedly spin round, like a Guinness clock, when Belle Rose touches them. They even have arms, and they give her an apple, a goblet, a comb, and a mirror. When distant fanfares (A) herald some change in the situation they blindfold Belle Rose. Then, creeping over the ground, comes a great green salamander; we hear his tune (B) superimposed over the strange Balinese sounds.

Suddenly the music quickens, the salamander casts his skin, and the Prince himself is revealed (J on the trumpets). He dances a *pas de deux* with the still blindfolded Belle Rose.

Before this broad tune dominates the music we hear some long, decorative melodies, largely based on the first three notes of the tune, first on the cor anglais and then on the flute (over an accompaniment on the harp). When Belle Rose can bear the suspense no longer she tears off the bandage from her eyes, finds herself alone, hunts anxiously for she knows not what, and then, to her horror, finds behind one of the pagodas the great green salamander (gong, and B loud on the brass). She runs distressed from his attempted embraces, and the act ends quietly with more of the queer, mysterious gamelan sounds (with B superimposed).

Act III

Scene 1: The Court of the Empress of the Middle Kingdom

We are back in the Emperor's palace, but the opening music (G, and its companion, the long, slowly rising theme over a persistent bass) shows that Belle Épine is now in control. Her arrogance is now beyond all bounds. She summons the Emperor, her father, and he is carried in in a cage (like one of the captive monarchs in Marlowe's *Tamburlaine*), wretched and miserable. He is forced to dance to a pathetic tune on the saxophone.

A very quiet episode for muted horns and oboes, deriving from D, is headed in the score, "I was once an Emperor." Suddenly Belle Rose runs in, exhausted and in rags; we hear both her falling tune, and the forlorn oboe melody (H). She is followed by the salamander; the orchestra draws our attention to him (B), but for the moment he remains unnoticed at the back. Belle Rose tries to console her father (Q in a new rhythm; cut on the record), but almost at once Belle Épine orders the guards to seize her sister (G, imperious and a little flustered). The salamander comes forward to save her, and he too is seized. To the tune of the *pas de deux* in Act II (P) Belle Rose, touched by the salamander's self-sacrifice, forgets her horror of the creature and tenderly embraces him, imploring the guards to leave him alone. Her love overcomes the spell that has been placed on him (one remembers the tale of *Beauty and the Beast*), and in a clap of thunder the Prince springs from the discarded salamander skin, and the palace disappears into darkness.

The orchestra now provides an interlude; at first slowly and quietly, it embroiders the Prince's themes (B and J) against gamelan music, which suggests that we shall soon return to the Kingdom of the Pagodas; the music builds up to a fine climax.

Scene 2: Belle Rose's Triumphant Return and Marriage to the Prince of the Pagodas

The story of the ballet is now over. After some fanfares (A and J) the final scene consists of a *divertissement*, in which various unspecified people dance for the entertainment of the Prince and his bride (and also of the Emperor and the faithful Fool, who have followed Belle Rose). The Prince and Belle Rose naturally return the compliment in a big *pas de deux*. But first comes the *pas de six*, which consists of

Entrée. A cheerful piece, with a charming, syncopated, contrasting tune played by the oboe.
Variation 1 (Boy and Girl). A fine, broad tune for horns, accompanied on the piano.

Variation 2 (Girl). A quick violin solo in six-eight time.
Variation 3 (Boy). A quick, vigorous waltz.
Variation 4. A piece for three of the six dancers, with a most engaging tune. Underneath the notes I have given a rough indication of the bass accompaniment.

Coda. (This has been rewritten since the ballet was first performed; the record gives neither version.)

Next, after a short *pas de caractère* for the Emperor and the Fool (not on the record), the Prince and Belle Rose dance their big *pas de deux*:

A long, majestic, and energetic piece for both dancers.
The Prince's variation.

Belle Rose's variation (U)—regrettably truncated at Covent Garden. Again I have given a
rough indication of the bass.

In the middle section the orchestra lovingly recalls Q.

There being no coda, the Finale follows immediately. After an introduction (based on
J, treated fugally), it consists for the most part of a cheerful waltz in rondo form, in which
many of the tunes return (though in some cases much disguised). The first theme is an
ingenious amalgam of the various elements that make up the Prince's tune (J).

Almost at once we hear (though it is easily missed) Belle Rose's theme (H) on the violins;
both V and H are heard over the simplest of um-cha-cha accompaniments. Then we
hear R as some of the *pas de six* dancers come in. (Next, Q should be played by the tuba,
to signify the old Emperor's return, but this is now cut at Covent Garden.) S follows, and
then V. All these tunes are forced into the waltz rhythm of the Finale.

In the final Apotheosis we hear for the last time the fanfares (A), the salamander tune
(B), raised to the height of grandeur, and, very briefly at the very end, the Fool's gay scale
runs as he joins the hands of the Prince and the Princess. This unpretentious, frivolous
ending is wholly delightful; it contains more than a hint of the ending of *Der Rosenkavalier*.

It scarcely needs saying that many influences have contributed to *The Prince of the Pagodas*.
It does perhaps need saying that where I have drawn attention to these my comments are
not intended to carry any critical stigma. It does not seem possible that anyone will ever
produce a new full-length ballet which is quite free from the influence of previous full-
length ballets or other stage works. Indeed, the choreographer and composer who studiously
avoid such influences are highly unlikely to produce anything of the slightest value. *The
Prince of the Pagodas* seems to me an intelligent and interesting mixture of the old and the new.

Chapter Eight
CODETTA

If this book has a moral it is that the ballet with the best chance of immortality is the
one with the best music. A ballet with wonderful dancing and poor music may give just as
much pleasure over a short period of time, perhaps even more, but it has little or no hope
of survival. A case in point is the Festival Ballet's *Études*, to music by Czerny. The choreography is tailor-made for a company with very great technical ability, and the result is an
astonishing *tour de force* that brings the house down. Artistically, the piece seems to have
nothing to offer. The décor is unambitious to a degree, while the music is incredibly banal.
If I venture to predict that this ballet will not last I do not intend to condemn it as worth-
less. There have always been ballets aiming at technical display and little more, and I
hope there always will be, in due proportion. But I am here discussing those ballets which

form the immortal core of the repertoire; in my opinion these are never merely concerned with technical display. The whole history of ballet suggests that audiences are not prepared to watch the same steps over and over again *unless* they are accompanied by music which, in a trite phrase, "grows on you." In other words, there must be something of artistic substance in the non-choreographic constituents of ballet. Only the very best composers and the very best artists are good enough. It has recently been suggested that the very best poets might also be approached. Most of the ballets in this book have themes that can be described as fundamentally poetic. Might not the modern poet have new ideas to contribute—something fresh on which choreographer and composer can work? These fresh ideas must be simple ones; ballet is no medium for existentialism, in my opinion. But it is certain that fresh themes are badly needed to prevent ballet going round in circles, and it may well be that poets would prove the most fruitful source.

Appendix

LIST OF RECORDINGS

ALP, CLP, and DLP are H.M.V. records; LXT, Decca; MRL, Mercury

ADAM, ADOLPHE

Giselle. (*a*) Covent Garden Orchestra, conducted by Robert Irving (DLP 1004): a selection of ten numbers. (*b*) Orchestre du Théâtre National de l'Opéra, conducted by Richard Blareau (LXT 2844): a potted French version based on the Busser arrangement.

BRITTEN, BENJAMIN

The Prince of the Pagodas. Covent Garden Orchestra, conducted by Benjamin Britten (LXT 5336-37): some cuts.

DELIBES, LÉO

Coppélia. (*a*) L'Orchestre de la Suisse Romande, conducted by Ernest Ansermet (LXT 5342-43): complete. (*b*) Covent Garden Orchestra, conducted by Robert Irving (CLP 1046): about half the ballet has been cut. *Sylvia.* Philharmonia Orchestra, conducted by Robert Irving (CLP 1058): much cut.

RAVEL, MAURICE

Daphnis and Chloe. (*a*) Geneva Choir, L'Orchestre de la Suisse Romande, conducted by Ernest Ansermet (LXT 2775): complete. (*b*) New England Conservatory Chorus, Boston Symphony Orchestra, conducted by Charles Münch (ALP 1374): complete.

STRAVINSKY, IGOR

The Firebird. L'Orchestre de la Suisse Romande, conducted by Ernest Ansermet (LXT 5115): complete. There are several recordings of the Suite taken from this ballet. *Petrushka.* L'Orchestre de la Suisse Romande, conducted by Ernest Ansermet (LXT 5375): complete. There are several other good complete recordings.

TCHAIKOVSKY, PETER

Nutcracker. Minneapolis Symphony Orchestra, conducted by Antal Dorati (MRL 2508-9): complete. *The Sleeping Beauty.* (*a*) Minneapolis Symphony Orchestra, conducted by Antal Dorati (MRL 12524-27): complete. (*b*) Covent Garden Orchestra, conducted by Robert Irving (CLP 1073-74): more economical than (*a*) and better played; it contains nearly all the music used at Covent Garden. *Swan Lake.* (*a*) Minneapolis Symphony Orchestra, conducted by Antal Dorati (MRL 2528-30): the 1882 version complete. (*b*) London Symphony Orchestra, conducted by Anatole Fistoulari (LXT 2681-82): contains most of the music used at Covent Garden (Petipa's version).

VAUGHAN WILLIAMS, RALPH

Job. London Philharmonic Orchestra, conducted by Sir Adrian Boult (LXT 2937): complete.